CHAKRA
WORKOUT

CHAKRA
WORKOUT

Balancing Your Energy with Yoga and Meditation

Mary Horsley

Sterling Publishing Co., Inc.
New York

Library of Congress Cataloging-in-Publication Data Available

10 9 8 7 6 5 4 3 2 1

Published in 2007 by Sterling Publishing Co., Inc.
387 Park Avenue South, New York, NY 10016

First published in the UK by Gaia Books
A division of Octopus Publishing Group Ltd
© 2006 by Octopus Publishing Group Ltd
Text © 2006 by Mary Horsley

Distributed in Canada by Sterling Publishing
c/o Canadian Manda Group, 165 Dufferin Street
Toronto, Ontario, Canada M6K 3H6

Printed in China
All rights reserved

Sterling ISBN-13: 978-1-4027-3332-1
        ISBN-10: 1-4027-3332-1

For information about custom editions, special sales, premium and
corporate purchases, please contact Sterling Special Sales
Department at 800-805-5489 or specialsales@sterlingpub.com.

contents

a note from the author

As a little girl, growing up with four older brothers who made natural pairs of two, I spent a lot of time in a world of my own. When I wasn't dreaming of being center stage at Covent Garden during ballet class ("Mary Horsley, will you please wake up …") I talked to my imaginary sister-in-law, pet toad Trethias, Timmy the tortoise and the hens. At night, when I lay down to sleep I would regularly have what I called "my Alice feeling," when I would become aware of the world slowly turning in space. After a while it would feel as if my body twisted in one direction, my head in the other, and I spiraled out of my body, grew very tall and kind of extruded up to the ceiling. I didn't expect to be taken any more seriously about this event than about my imaginary sister-in-law, so I kept it secret, even though I found it rather frightening, and often wondered "what if I can't get back down again?" Ironically I now realize that my father, an unusual man— general practitioner, vegetarian, antivivisectionist and mystic—would probably have been able to tell me all about out-of-body experiences.

I first studied yoga in Swansea, on the south coast of Wales, in my late 20s. I'd been having a disagreement (OK, a row) with my three-year-old son in the village shop. I was paying when I heard a very calm lady explaining to him kindly that perhaps mummy didn't want to buy him that box of cereal because it was full of sugar and was not very good for him. Where did she get that calm? I wanted some. She told me about her yoga class.

One evening the teacher brought in a red peony for us to meditate on. Not long into the exercise I realized that the flower was pulsing out an unmistakable green light for about 1 inch (2.5 cm) all around its petals. I could hardly bear to wait for the end of the exercise to share what I had seen. My teacher was very wise, acknowledged my experience, but made light of it.

A few months later I lay on my stomach on the floor of the sitting room in front of the fire reading, in a type of cobra position, when I noticed that a shining silver crescent was superimposed on the page, like cut glass. I rubbed my eyes, but it didn't go away. I looked around the room; the crescent was everywhere I looked. I took out my contact lenses. The crescent was still there, bigger if anything. I even called the doctor. Hours later it faded away. It was many years later, when I was doing my yoga teacher training, I heard Swami Venkatesananda describe the symbol for Svadisthana chakra. I was stunned. He described exactly what I'd seen. From that moment on I developed a particular interest in the chakras and read every book I could find on them. Significantly, I realized that certain postures could trigger the spontaneous opening of a chakra.

When I studied acupuncture in the 1980s, we practiced looking at patients' faces to read the subtle colors around the eyes and mouth that indicate which meridians were imbalanced. I began to see people walking about with a glow around them. It became obvious to me that this "other dimension" was ever present—quite normal, in fact.

One day I had just needled a patient's foot when I noticed a line of light glowing along the pathway of the meridian. I didn't tell her what I saw, but instead asked her: "Can you see that?" She confirmed what I was seeing. "So that's how they discovered the pathways," I thought. I'd always wondered, not quite buying the traditional explanation of finding links between meridians and organs in wounded soldiers on the battlefield.

About ten years ago I was with a group receiving teaching from Geshe Lama Konchog in Kopan monastery in Kathmandu. We had been sitting cross-legged for hours. When we stood for him to leave we heard a resounding crack ricochet around the temple, and one of our party collapsed in agony. Several of us were therapists and rushed to her aid. It seemed that she had broken her ankle bone. To my great surprise, Geshe Lama, famed for his healing powers, gave us no more than a glance and left the temple for his rooms nearby. The next day we were due to go trekking in the Himalayas. The miracle was that this girl was among us, and her ankle was fully recovered.

We all have the potential to experience this other dimension and deepen our understanding. Far from being a space-case, I am very down to earth (unlike my younger self) with a healthy dose of skepticism—I only believe things if they check out. There was a time not that long ago when chakra teachings were kept secret, perhaps for fear of misuse of power. I know there is a built in safety net, and believe that they only fully open when you are ready to apply their power for the greater good.

I would like to dedicate this book to my yoga teacher, Fred Lock, as well as to all my students and patients who have taught me so much over the years I've known them. It is also for my children, Owen and Meg, their partners, Diana and Frank, my grandchildren, Nina, Nils and Indigo, and my late parents, Jim and Judy, with thanks for putting up with my weird ideas.

Mary Horsley/Sangye Khadro

introduction

Imagine standing quietly, naked, looking at yourself in a full-length mirror for several minutes. What would you see?

You would see your physical body, somewhat sculpted by the type of life you have led and the thoughts you hold. There may be temporary effects, such as tense shoulders, if you are going through a difficult time. Perhaps there would be a play of emotion on your face. Some of you may have smile or frown lines etched permanently into your skin; others may have a serene, smooth countenance. For the vast majority, what we would see is what/who we are—bones, flesh, muscles—arranged to our approval, or not.

What if I were to tell you that the reflection in the mirror is only half, maybe even less, of the true picture? How can you see the whole image?

Try this exercise: stand in front of a mirror in a dim light, breathe quietly for several minutes with your eyes closed. Now open them and stare for a long time at your image, letting your eyes slip out of focus (gazing less at your physical body, more at the immediate area surrounding it). You may get a surprise. And my guess is that if you do, you will want to rub your eyes in disbelief, and with that action, the image will disappear. When we look at ourselves, or anyone else, in the right frame of mind, and preferably in a half-light, we can become privy to the world of the subtle energies, which surround and interpenetrate our physical bodies, and see the aura of human consciousness.

The subtle energies and aura

These subtle energies are made in part from our life force, or prana, woven through our body in pathways or meridians (*meridian*, translated from the Chinese, means "warp") like an electric circuit. The yogis call these pathways the nadis (see pages 16–17). In addition, there is a surrounding field of energy, called the aura, extending out from the body. Color and light emanates from and interpenetrates this field from pools of concentrated energy aligned up the spine, from base to crown, like sparkling jewels on a necklace. These are known as the chakras.

For most people the aura at first looks like a rather ill-defined haze of whitish-gray light surrounding the body by just about 1 inch (2–3 cm) or so. With practice, we would see how it extends out from the body, and surrounds it in an eggshape (see right). And this is only the beginning …

The aura is multilayered, each layer interpenetrating the next, lain over our physical body like shades over a lamp, or Russian dolls. These layers are called the *koshas*, or sheaths, and together they make up our subtle force field of energy. The aura of a healthy person is lustrous, glowing, tinted with vibrant colors and shimmering with movement like a mirage. Its appearance changes with our moods, however, and it can be affected by the atmosphere around us.

Each individual chakra opens the door to a stage of development. As we grow, given the right conditions, each one unfolds in turn (they are traditionally represented as lotus blossoms) to support and reflect our development at that stage. We start the journey at birth with a concentration of energy in the base chakra, which is connected with feelings of security. The energy rises then through a focus on creativity, personal power,

Aura shape
The aura extending out from the body is roughly egg-shaped. With a highly spiritually evolved person the aura's shape is wider at the crown and pointed at the feet.

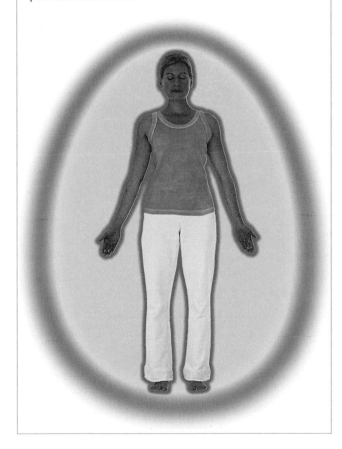

may move on in some respects, but have lasting issues with insecurity. This taints the aura, leaving a resonance, or damage, that is clearly visible to a clairvoyant. Red being the associated color of the first chakra, there may be a muddying of that color in the energy field, or a predominance or lack of red, particularly around the lower part of the aura. If we feel insecure, it shows up in our aura, and even if others don't see it, on some level they pick up on it.

Fortunately, it is possible to rebalance and heal the chakras, as we will see. By learning more about them and the areas of life and emotions they influence, you can work out which ones may need a little extra support and then take the necessary steps to heal and fine tune them. I suggest many enjoyable ways to do this throughout this book, particularly through the practice of yoga, various breathing techniques and meditation.

The chakras

Starting at the perineum and appearing in stages up the spine to the crown are the seven main chakras. *Chakra*, literally translated from Sanskrit, means "wheel." These whirling vortices of energy glow with the light of the spectrum, from red at the base to violet at the crown. The base chakra radiates light and energy downward, the next five predominantly forward, and the crown chakra upward. They communicate with each other via their common connection with the same nadi/channel, which rises centrally up the body with the spine, known as the Sushumna (see pages 16–17).

The balance of subtle energies in the chakras affects everything you think, say or do and this, in turn, affects the aura; the chakras refine your personality and how you present yourself to the world, having a definite influence on your physical appearance and the tendencies of your character. How often do you hear the expression that it is impossible to love someone else until you learn to love yourself? In the person who received the message at some stage that they were unlovable, the poor heart chakra may, to a clairvoyant, appear literally broken, the self-loathing being evident in the aura. To heal that wound, revitalizing the energy in the chakra would allow

compassion, communication, intuition and finally union with the divine, or bliss. Opening the chakras is like walking into a room where we have to learn a lesson, finding the key to the next, and so on. Opening each chakra raises our consciousness to the next level, thus increasing wholeness and allowing us to move on when we are ready.

Unfortunately, circumstances may not be conducive to the proper opening of a chakra, or they may even block it. We may not have been lucky enough to experience feeling secure as an infant, inhibiting that energetic support and opening of the first chakra, Muladhara. We

This 18th-century Indian miniature painting shows a yogi covered from head to foot in tatoos. It comes from a series portraying various yoga techniques.

them to feel compassion for themselves and, therefore, others, and to love unconditionally. That would be truly transforming.

The chakras provide a vitalizing force to your physical body. You could, in a way, regard them as the pressure valves of the subtle-energy system, discharging energy and color out into your surrounding force field. Fall in love and your aura will glow green—the color of the heart chakra. We can all feel that special energy around a person who is newly in love.

About this book

Since the chakras have such a powerful influence on all aspects of our lives, there is enormous benefit to be gained from taking the time to balance them. Over the years I have devised many methods of working on the chakras, applying my knowledge of the meridians and yoga. Chapter 1 of this book describes the aura in detail and takes you on a comprehensive journey through the seven main chakras and their associations, which you will find in Chapter 2. You will learn many practical ways to balance them including the use of color, sound, mantras, aromatherapy oils, crystals, massage and food. I have not included astrological associations, since I have yet to meet astrologer colleagues who agree on the same associations. In Chapter 3 I describe some of the important minor chakras and their associations.

Chapter 4 describes asanas, or yoga postures, for the chakras and lists the benefits of each one. Yoga is one of the most potent ways I have found to work on rebalancing your chakras and its practice brings many other benefits as well. Many people experience the powerful effect yoga has on their lives beyond just the physical, without realizing why it is so effective. Without knowing it, they have been rebalancing their chakras. Learning how the postures affect the chakras and then applying that knowledge to your practice greatly enhances its efficacy, and provides you with an extra tool to achieve emotional balance. There are the dual benefits of improving physical health in an enjoyable way (it is great fun doing the postures) at the same time as developing a calm mind and a positive attitude to life—and you can do it independently without having to pay huge sums of money to a therapist!

By using the correct breathing technique with the yoga postures, and practicing various powerful breathing techniques, which are described in Chapter 5, you will greatly speed progress, raising energy levels through all the chakras.

Finally, in Chapter 6, you will find meditation techniques integral to a properly balanced yoga practice, helping to calm the mind and bringing great clarity and a deep spiritual dimension to your growth.

The image of the lotus flower is used for all the chakras.

1 | the aura

There is a state in which it is possible to enjoy perfect health, never to be ruffled by emotions (ours or other people's) and everything, including the past and future, is known and understood at the deepest level. While it is rare for this state of enlightenment to be reached, it is possible for each and every one of us to achieve it in this lifetime. But in order for this to happen, we need to have balanced and fully open chakras. The chakras are part of our subtle energy system, from which pools of concentrated life force radiate out through an aura, or human energy field, that surrounds us (see pages 8–9).

A clairvoyant looking at us might be able to see a light show of blending color shimmering around our bodies in radiating rings, tinted by each chakra and affected by our thoughts, emotions, lifestyle, behavior and activities. The human aura varies greatly from person to person, mood to mood, and can be read as both a "current account" and a biography of our lives.

With yoga it is possible to brighten and clear the aura, which, over the years, becomes damaged by the normal ups and downs of life. Another benefit of yoga is that it extends the aura farther out, forming a protective field of radiant light. The postures, or asanas, retune the chakras so that each spins strongly in the correct direction and communicates well with the others.

Instinctive recognition

We influence our aura, and other people's, whether we are conscious of it or not. Animals have auras and react instinctively to those they encounter, avoiding some while being drawn to others. In more attuned cultures, so-called "primitive peoples" could see auras and often depicted them in their art. Nowadays, most of us have lost this knack, but you have probably already experienced the human energy field without knowing it. Remember that feeling of finding yourself next to someone you want to get away from? Something about

them warns you to keep your distance. Or perhaps you know someone whose very presence makes you feel good, they "light up a room."

Balanced and unbalanced auras

The aura of a balanced person is beautiful: luminous, vibrating and spiraling, a constant interplay of light and subtle colors. In a deeply spiritual person, there is a predominance of luminous lilac-blue, and there may even be sparkling golden stars around the crown. The colors in the aura are beyond the normal range the eye can see: there are said to be more than 1,400 shades of blue, 1,000 reds, 1,400 browns, 800 greens, 550 oranges, 360 violets and 12 whites.

In people with unbalanced chakras, the aura is often clouded by emotion, with chaotic whirlpools and cross-currents, tainted with the smudgy blacks and browns of negative emotions. For example, instead of showing the pale, luminous blue-green of compassion, it may show the slimy gray-green of deceit. Anger shows as deep-red flashes on a black background; jealousy as scarlet flashes on a greenish-brown background. Since all our thoughts and emotions are reflected in our aura, it follows that its size, clarity and luminosity depend on how much mastery we have gained over our emotions and on the balance of energy in the chakras themselves.

The human energy field

The aura extends out from our bodies in layers of radiant light in an egg shape. This is an illustration of how you may first see auras. (The symbols of the seven main chakras are superimposed on the picture to show their location.) A clairvoyant sees more and reads the state of the chakras from the way their associated colors appear in the aura.

layers of the aura

A human being has three separate, but interpenetrating "bodies," known as the koshas, or sheaths, which make up the aura. These bodies are the gross/physical body, known as the *annamaya kosha*; the subtle body or etheric double (consisting of the astral and two mental bodies), known as the *suk-ma-ar-ra*; and the causal/spiritual body, known as the *karana sarira*. In Tantric (transcendental) yoga, the layers that make up these bodies are sometimes called the cosmic folds, or the five envelopes. From the physical body outward to the causal body, the layers decrease in density and increase in luminosity, all but the physical body forming the aura.

1 Annamaya kosha
Physical body

The physical body as we know it is associated with the elements of the lowest three chakras: Muladhara (earth), Svadisthana (water) and Manipura (fire), which are treated in detail in Chapter Two (see pages 24–31, 32–9 and 40–7). At the same time, the physical body is also interwoven with prana/energy, penetrating right inside it from the next sheath, the pranayama kosha. Prana, or life force, is transported throughout the body in thousands of channels, known as the nadis, or meridians. In a way, it is as if our physical body is woven on warps of human electricity that invisibly keep it together.

2 Pranayama kosha
Astral body/etheric double

The astral body comprises not only the prana of the nadis, which surrounds all systems, but also the full astral/pranic body, extending 10–12 inches (25–30 cm) beyond the physical body and forming the second sheath. In the moral or intellectual person, it extends outward up to 18 inches (45 cm)—farther still in spiritually evolved individuals. It is affected by our emotions, passions and desires and by our thoughts. It is the first 1 inch (2.5 cm) of the astral sheath that looks like a hazy version of a person (known as the etheric double or *doppelgänger*), which is sometimes seen as a phantom after death. The astral body relates to Anahata chakra (see pages 48–55) and Vishuddha chakra (see pages 56–63). It appears starry and luminous to muddy and coarse, depending on the development of the person.

The astral body responds positively to being fed with constructive feelings, thoughts, aspirations and selfless love, and without which it slowly wears away. It allows us to experience sensations/feelings and provides a bridge between the mental and the physical bodies.

3 Manomaya kosha
First sheath of the mind

The first kosha of the mind carries our concrete thoughts, such as: "this is a book." It is interpenetrated by prana, which gives these thoughts energy. It relates, as above, to Anahata and Vishuddha chakras. Rotating on its axis, it displays bands of color throughout the structure—not so much coloring our thoughts as displaying the color of our thoughts.

4 Vijnanamaya kosha
Second sheath of the mind

Relating to the higher mind, this luminous kosha relates to abstract ideas and thoughts such as literature, for example, or the meaning of life. Vijnanamaya kosha is highly active during the dreaming state. Although we are unaware of its activity most of the time, it can be strengthened by practicing lucid dreaming techniques. This kosha can provide us with many insights if we practice recording our dreams in a diary immediately on waking. It is associated with Ajna chakra (see pages 64–9), the seat of intuition.

The aura of the mind koshas is delicate and has a rapid motion of particles, like living, iridescent light. Together these mental sheaths show flashes of colors like shot silk, varying from the violet-blue (at the top of the aura) of aspirational thoughts, a narrow blue ring of devotional thought at neck level, a crimson to rose-pink or green band at heart level of affectionate thoughts, golden-yellow at abdomen level of philosophical thoughts and so on. They usually link to the spectrum of the chakras rising up the body, and reflect the quality of energy present in each one.

5 Anandamaya kosha/Karana sarira
Causal body

Extremely rarefied and fine, this, the outermost sheath of joy or bliss, receives cosmic energy from the universal field that surrounds all things. Gaze at a tree against a clear blue sky and you will soon see an aura glowing mainly green around it. And if you look a little longer you might see squiggles of energy entering its aura. A cut leaf shows a break in its aura and an immediate inrush of energy from this universal field to heal it. The Anandamaya kosha is our receiver of this universal healing energy.

The causal body relates to the crown chakra, Sahasrara (see pages 70–5). In a spiritually evolved person, it is colored pale blue with shades of violet—the color of Sahasrara—displaying the state of non-duality or bliss. This sheath carries stored within it, like the invisible hard drive of a computer, the cause for our present incarnation (hence its name), and the complete information on all our past lives. To some of us, this is revealed as we die; in the enlightened, it is already known. In most people, the causal body is not fully developed, while in the Buddha it was said to extend nearly 3 miles (5 km).

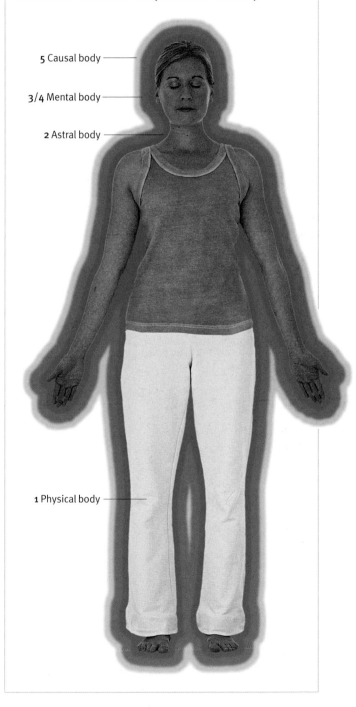

Different layers of the human aura
The layers of the aura vary in size, depending on the development of the person. The density of the layers decreases the farther they are from the body.

5 Causal body

3/4 Mental body

2 Astral body

1 Physical body

the nadis

Let us take a closer look at the subtle energy system. While we have seven main chakras aligned up the spine, we actually have many thousands of minor chakras throughout our bodies. These are like pools where energy eddies in the thousands of pathways where prana/subtle energy flows. These nadis/meridians are said to number some 72,000, and one—the Sushumna—carries energy from one chakra to another, as described below. The translation of the Chinese word for *meridian* is "warp," as in the warp and weft of fabric—describing the way that we are interwoven in energy/light. They are the part of the second layer/sheath of the aura that also penetrates into the body (see Pranayama kosha, page 14).

The main energy currents

Like the twin serpents of the caduceus, the legendary herald's wand of the Greek god Hermes, the energy currents of Ida and Pingala twine themselves around the staff-like Sushumna. The Sushumna follows the path of the spine, connecting all the main chakras and allowing them to communicate.

The yoga postures, chants, meditations, pranayama, the food we eat, the air we breathe and the company we keep affects the prana/energy in the nadis, helping to balance and increase their flow. The function of the nadis is to absorb prana, to throw off toxins or waste and to activate Kundalini (see page 18). Each meridian reflects the health, emotional and physical, of our organs. These, in turn, affect the chakras, and finally our aura. If our heart is broken, the heart meridian may flag up trouble along its pathway with pain along the arm. It may also discolor the aura radiating out from the heart chakra, close it down, block it or reduce its rate of spin.

You cannot dissect a nadi and put it on a plate, any more than you can dissect an electrical current. To most people they are invisible, but they have been seen by clairvoyants and were illustrated in ancient texts all over the Far East. I have seen a meridian glowing with light (see page 7) and am convinced that this is how the ancient peoples mapped the meridians in the first place.

The most important nadis connected with the chakra system are the three main currents—the Sushumna, Ida and Pingala, which coil around the chakras, and each other to divide at the brow chakra.

Sushumna

This is the main energy current. It travels up the spine from the base chakra, or Muladhara, starting at the perineum for men and the cervix for women, and finishes at the crown of the head in the region of the fontanelle. It receives yang/Shiva energy from the heavens and seeks to unite with the yin/Shakti energy from the earth.

Ida

The left-sided current of energy, starting on the left of the perineum and ending at the left nostril, Ida is sometimes called *Ganga*, after the life-sustaining, purifying properties of the river Ganges. Left-nostril breathing can be used beneficially for all quiet, focused activities, such as writing, and other pursuits that give stability to life. Deliberately using left-nostril breathing during the day helps to balance yang nature. Ida energy is most predominant during the period from new moon to full. This is when the moon grows like a pregnant belly—a good time to build on projects that are already started.

Associations
- Female (yin) energy
- Sattvic (calm) tendencies
- Left side
- Left eye
- Left-nostril breath
- Lunar current
- Nourishing
- Purifying by water
- Shakti

Pingala

The right-sided current of energy beginning on the right of the perineum and ending at the right nostril is known as Pingala. It is rajasic (energizing or active) in nature, making the body more dynamic and efficient, and is more rational. Right-nostril breathing helps us to achieve more dynamic, active tasks. Sleeping while lying on the left side at night (which opens the right nostril) stops us burning off energy in dreams, increasing vitality and longevity. It is said that "the night is the day of the yogis": in other words, a very potent time to use energies such as these. Pingala energy is most active in the period from the full moon to new moon, and it can help us to initiate new projects.

Associations
- Male (yang) energy
- Rajasic (energetic) tendencies
- Right side
- Right eye
- Right-nostril breath
- Solar current
- Activity
- Purifying by fire
- Shiva

kundalini

The divine power,
Kundalini shines
like the stem of a young lotus;
like a snake, coiled round upon herself,
she holds her tail in her mouth
and lies resting half asleep
at the base of the body.
—Yoga Kundalini Upanishad (1.82)

Kundalini is the name for the powerful transcendental energy that lies dormant, like a snake coiled in the basin of the pelvis, ready to rise up the Sushumna and activate the seven main chakras. If there is a block in any one of the main chakras, Kundalini cannot fully rise and unite yin energy from the earth and yang from the universal field in order to bring about enlightenment.

People report different experiences of Kundalini rising—it can be a sudden, shocking movement, or it can feel much more subtle. If the earth element is predominant, it may feel like a creeping sensation in the Sushumna, like an ant. If water is predominant, it feels like the sensation of a hopping frog, or a throbbing. If the energy rising up the Sushumna feels burning hot—a sensation like a fiery stream—it indicates that the fire element, Agni, is predominant. When the air element is predominant, the feeling can be more like a fluttering bird or a lightness in the heart region.

When many of the chakras are awoken at the same time, and the element of Akasha/ether is predominant, the feeling can be a more shocking experience. Energy rises dramatically up the Sushumna to the crown in one sudden movement, opening the chakras spontaneously as it goes, as if sleeping Kundalini was struck a blow with a stick.

Although the exercises in this book may raise Kundalini, it is good to put that thought aside, for if anything will block its passage more surely it is expectation. It is better to pay attention to the basics with humility, and allow what will happen to happen.

Kundalini means "coiling"—energy and consciousness coiling and looping as a snake.

The force is latent within us all, and can be encouraged with patient work on the chakras and by living life ethically (see the eightfold path, page 21). Kundalini may attempt to rise and retreat many times before completing the journey to the crown chakra. The possibility of this happening depends on how balanced and open our chakras are, and whether we are strong enough or sufficiently emotionally prepared for all that enlightenment brings.

the bandhas

Energy can sometimes be focused in a particular area of the
Sushumna, which is the main energy current that travels up the
spine, or on a particular chakra by applying what are known as
"bandhas," or energy locks. These bandhas/locks are often
added to yoga postures, called asanas, and encourage Kundalini
to rise. One such asana, maha mudra, applies all three locks
with powerful effect (see page 129).

Mula bandha
Anal lock
A contraction of muscles in the perineum, around the
anus. The effect is to draw base chakra energy upward,
reversing its flow and concentrating it in the Sushumna
(see Muladhara, pages 98–100).

Uddiyana bandha
Abdominal lock
Drawing up energy by a strong contraction of the
abdomen (see Manipura, pages 106–9).

Jalandhara bandha
Chin lock
Taking the chin down to the hollow between the
chest and the neck by stretching the neck and
contracting the throat (see right). This stops the
downward flow of subtle nectar/fluid, known
as soma, from the cavity between the two
hemispheres of the brain and is said
to revitalize the whole organism
and promote longevity.

the granthis

There are three significant blocks, or psychic hurdles, we must cross in order to raise energy in the Sushumna. These are known in Tantric terminology as the *granthis*, or knots. They arise at various levels in the chakras, and will block energy rising any higher up the Sushumna until the required work on that chakra is complete.

Rudra granthi

Vishnu granthi

Brahma granthi

Brahma granthi

More usually said to be located at the position of the base, or Muladhara chakra, the brahma granthi is sometimes placed at the navel. This granthi is responsible for keeping us attached to earthly objects and sensations and it is related to the physical body. When this knot is untied we can master the mind (see also page 140).

Vishnu granthi

Located at Anahata chakra, in the region of the heart, untying the vishnu granthi frees us from worldly attachment to compassion and devotion, and unites us with cosmic faith. It is related to the astral body and the world of emotions (see page14–15).

Rudra granthi

Located in the area of the third eye, Ajna chakra, this knot takes us beyond the five elements to become *tattvatita*— free of time-bound consciousness, unfettered by time and space, able to appear in any place at any time and having many extraordinary powers. The rudra granthi is related to the causal body, to thoughts, visions and intuitions.

A danger lies here in becoming lost in the world of miraculous powers (*siddis*) and intuitions and, thus, blocking farther progress.

patanjali's eightfold path

Successful progress in your yoga practice and learning to balance the energy in the chakras depend on following the ancient eightfold path, like logical steps on a ladder, laid out by yogic master Patanjali in his *Hatha Yoga Pradipika*. These are known as the "eight limbs of yoga." Intended to shape your attitude so that you may grow and develop, mastering the first steps makes progress much easier.

Yamas

Behaving with restraint: nonviolent, truthful, honest and kind; eating moderately, being straightforward, acting with forbearance, fortitude and being sexually continent. In other words, purity of thought, words and deeds.

Niyamas

Having a spiritual, charitable, devotional attitude, including things such as modesty, prayer, discernment, worship and austerity.

Asanas

Practicing the yoga postures/asanas regularly, with a view to being able to hold a meditation posture comfortably still for extended periods. When the posture is steady, so is the mind.

Pranayama

Developing prana/breath control—with the postures, and as a separate practice.

Pratyahara

Learning to control the senses so that they do not disturb, and to prepare the mind for practicing visualization and concentration.

Dharana

Concentration—learning one-pointedness of the mind.

Dhyana

Practicing regular meditation so that the inner dialogue ceases and you become calm and undisturbed by interrupting thoughts.

Samadhi

The final goal: bliss/transcendent consciousness. Freedom from duality.

Taking the first steps

This book is laid out with respect for Patanjali's path. The chances are that if you have picked it up and have showed an interest, then you have already taken the first two steps. You may already be adept at the postures and want to add depth to your practice, or you may be completely new to yoga. Either way, I hope you enjoy the journey as much as I continue to do.

2 the seven main chakras

The word *chakra* comes from the Sanskrit word that translates as "wheel"—a reference to the seven principal energy vortices spinning like wheels, and which are aligned with the spine centrally up the body. The seven main chakras are where prime concentrations of chi/prana emanate from the central core of our bodies and project outward. The chakras can be likened to a series of doorways with keys to our development through life, and are clearly visible to some clairvoyants, although knowledge of them used to be withheld from laypeople, partly because the subtleties of the system are not that easy to communicate in words, and partly out of respect for their power. True understanding of the chakras can be gained only experientially.

How the chakras radiate

Light spirals outward from each chakra in a vortex. From the front they look like spinning discs of colored light, but from the side they radiate in a funnel of spiraling light (like a small twister). As you can see they stem from deep within the body, are aligned with the spine and interconnect via a central channel, the Sushumna. The lowest chakra, Muladhara radiates downward connecting us to the earth, its element. The next five radiate forward, and the Sahasrara, the crown chakra, radiates upward to the heavens.

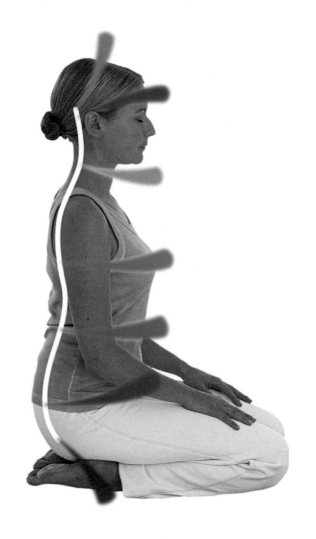

Locating the main chakras

Crown chakra
on and slightly above the crown

Brow chakra
at middle of the brow

Throat chakra
on the center of the throat

Heart chakra
on the middle of the chest

Solar plexus chakra
two finger-widths above
and below the navel

Sacral chakra
on and slightly
above the genitals

Root chakra
at the base of the spine

muladhara gateway of earth

MULA = ROOT *ADHARA* = SUPPORT

Location
Perineum

Purpose
Security, self-preservation

Color
Red

Element
Earth

Symbol
A yellow square with
four red petals

Age
Birth—7 or 8 years of age

Mantra
Lam

Vowel
Uh, as in cup

Balanced energy
Secure
Earthy
Attuned with nature
Generous
Trusting
Vital
Physical
Purposeful
Sensual
Active

**Unbalanced or blocked
energy**
Insecure
Fearful
Distrusting
Out of touch with nature
Indulgent
Exploitative
Materialistic
Rigid
Lethargic
Possessive

Location

More usually described as being found "in the perineum," or at the tip of the coccyx, the most precise location of Muladhara chakra is in the center of the perineum in men, between the anus and testicles, and at the tip of the cervix in women. Muladhara chakra usually projects red light/energy downward toward the ground. Kundalini practices (see page 18) seek to reverse this direction, raising energy up through the other chakras to the crown chakra, Sahasrara. This is also the root of Ida and Pingala energy (see pages 16–17), yin/ yang forces that spiral around the chakras and the central Sushumna.

Purpose

The purpose of Muladhara is security and self-preservation. Our journey up the chakras starts here, where this chakra anchors us securely to the ground, like the roots of a tree. Every sitting posture activates Muladhara. On those days when you feel unsupported by the world, focusing on the connection between your buttocks and the chair, be it in a meeting or waiting to see the dentist, can produce the support of Muladhara chakra.

The most basic needs of a newborn infant are for shelter, drink and food: Muladhara benefits from receiving those primary requirements. Beyond this, the infant also needs loving arms and tender care in order to grow and thrive. A study of chimpanzees, which had all their needs met apart from that last one of love and tenderness, saw them deteriorate and become severely depressed.

As adults, we need balanced energy in Muladhara, which governs self-preservation and the "fight-or-flight" response, to survive. A deer grazing in the wild is constantly on the lookout for danger. We need to find the balance between the type of constant fear that dominates us to the point of paranoia, and healthy caution. Muladhara enables us to rise above the domination of fear and to experience it appropriately, to make an inner shift and transcend primitive fears.

Muladhara chakra also connects us with our tribal energy as well as to the collective unconscious. We all have a tribe—it's called "family." From a very young age we learn its laws, such as "you get out of life what you put in" or "do as you would be done by." Balancing energy in Muladhara helps us to discriminate between destructive codes and those that are helpful. Believing "our family is not academic" or "little girls should be seen and not heard" is not going to serve you well. Family codes imbibed with mother's milk may carry the weight of many generations, but may also carry the delusions.

There is a karmic component to Muladhara energy. The blueprint we arrived with first engages with energy here. This relates to our material form, the physical body. We inherit physical characteristics, big noses or small feet, along with mental attitudes. It could be

said that each lifetime gives us the chance to challenge long-held attitudes, that we may have chosen our parents to set the scene for this change. The transformative energy of the chakras provides us with choice, the opportunity for a more evolved consciousness.

While the energy in Muladhara vibrates at the lowest, most dense level, we should never underestimate its importance as a force for grounding and stabilizing. This is especially important to remember when we undertake a journey of raising energy through the chakras. Some well-known spiritual leaders have fallen victim to neglect of the lower chakras, and lost discrimination as a result. We need to maintain a sound grounding in Muladhara from the start, and all through our practice.

This is the location of the brahma granthi (see page 20), the so-called "Knot of Brahma." It is as if we are given a golden/alchemical key at the door of each chakra that enables us to move on, but a granthi still tied keeps a bolt on the door, thus blocking our route forward. Until it is released we cannot achieve one-pointedness and meditate effectively, our minds are restless, uncontrolled, inconsistent and we are overly egotistical and ambitious. Following Patanjali's eightfold path (see page 21) helps us to release this knot, the grip of the ego, and in so doing to dissolve the illusions that are present at this first stage of our journey.

Muladhara is the abode of Kundalini, Shakti energy, which lies coiled here like a dormant snake (see page 18).

Color

Muladhara glows a clear bright red, like the fiery core of the planet (its color reminding us that the associated element is earth). I had a patient once who often arrived in a red coat saying: "I feel fit to face the world when I wear this." She intuitively chose the color that would make her feel secure. When you feel you need it, wear red—better still, wear red underpants. Light a red candle or sit in the glow of a red light bulb.

Element

The element associated with this chakra is earth. The foundation for the symbol for Muladhara is a yellow square, representing sustaining Earth. The stability of our homes depends on stable foundations, as do we. When the energy in Muladhara is balanced we feel safe and supported and are respectful of the Earth. We are secure enough to welcome change, feeling we will be supported by mother Earth, trusting that the next meal will come. (There is a whole generation of people fed on a strictly four-hourly basis—left to cry if the big hand wasn't on 2, 6 or 10—who now have issues with food.)

The art of feng shui places great importance on feeling secure at home. Fixing anything about your home that is broken—a cracked window pane, leaking tap and so on—will stop energy being leached out of Muladhara.

Sense

This chakra governs our ability to smell. Very much an underrated sense in modern society, it was once crucial to our survival. Before there were "best before" or "sell by" dates, we used our noses to tell us if food was safe to eat. Smell kept us clean by making us avoid our own waste products; it led us to our prey. Smell protects us from fire, alerts us to a kettle boiling dry and leads us to water.

This sense is constantly challenged in our almost pathologically deodorized and overscented society. Smell can give us very reliable information about our fellow humans, an ability that is all but lost nowadays. Chinese medics have used odors diagnostically for the last 5,000 years. They indicate which element is out of balance, the level of a patient's sickness, which emotion

The symbol of Muladhara

The yellow square (yantra/symbol) represents the goddess Priviti (her name means "the wide earth"). Arrows point out from the square in four directions, representing the possibilities life offers and the choices we have about the direction we take in life. They point into four red petals, each containing a Sanskrit symbol.

Next we find a white elephant, Airavata. Muladhara chakra is also connected with an ox or a bull. This chakra reminds us of our instinctive animal nature. An elephant is strong and intelligent, but it can also be wild and destructive—as can our minds. Airavata has a tether around his neck, and seven trunks, which represent the minerals necessary for physical life. (Astrophysicists grew excited when they discovered the same minerals present on Saturn's moon Titan that are also present on our planet Earth, indicating the possibility of life on that world, too.)

An arrow, or trikona, points down toward Airavata, representing Shakti energy, the feminine aspect of creation. Within this is a lingam, or phallus, which represents male, Shiva, energy. Coiled three and a half times around the lingam is a snake, representing the Kundalini force; tail in mouth, dormant, but with the potential to shoot up the spine when awakened.

Crowning the lingam is a tiny crescent moon, a citkala, symbolizing the divine source of all energy. At the top of the square are the deities Brahma and Dakini (see right).

Altogether, the symbol reminds us of the power of creation, the cosmic forces of yin/yang, male/female, that can be awakened with spiritual practise and used for transcendence.

Deities—Brahma and Dakini

It is traditional for each chakra to have a representation of a divine pair within its symbol. Here we have representations of Brahma as a child, with his consort, Dakini. They teach us of the possibilities that are present in Muladhara energy and we can use their images to contemplate these.

Brahma is depicted here in the form of a child, indicating the relative immaturity of consciousness at this level. The objects in his hands represent the lessons that need to be learned in Muladhara.

His danda, or staff, represents the spine, through which Kundalini energy may rise up through the body.

The gourd drinking cup represents slaking spiritual thirst.

His rosary is a string of 108 beads, and represents the many names of Shakti, the divine feminine aspect.

He makes a gesture, holding up his hand, palm facing forward, for dispelling fear.

Dakini carries a spear, relating to the ability to direct our energy toward targets.

The sword she carries relates to the power of discrimination, held here with palm forward to dispel fear.

The staff with a skull on the top relates to the state of an empty mind.

The cup contains the water of life, from which the aspirant hopes to drink.

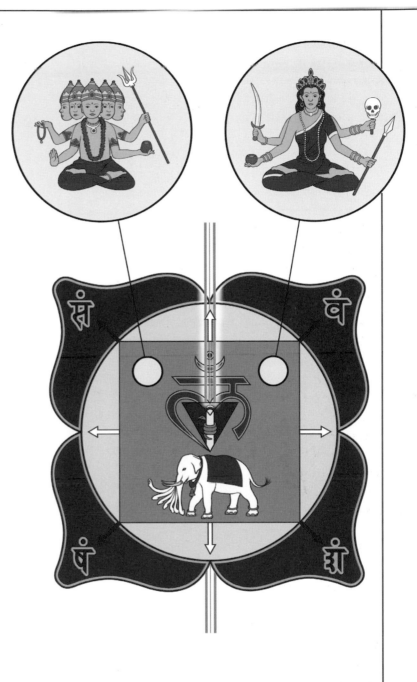

is predominant and which might cause problems, both physical and psychological. If the earth element is out of balance, patients smelled fragrant, alerting me to look at their stomach and spleen meridians and to enquire how they were mothered.

You can retrain this sense and activate Muladhara at the same time. Never, for example, pass a rose bush without taking a deep sniff. Smell food before you eat it to see if it makes your mouth water. Light incense or use fragrant oils in a burner. Sniff your dog's or cat's paws when they have been running on wet grass.

Age

This chakra is strongest from birth to about 7 or 8 years of age. When we are tiny infants, all that matters to us is that our immediate physical and emotional needs are met. In most instances, a silent baby would not thrive— indeed, a passive, silent baby is one that alerts us to the presence of sickness. We cry to be fed, to have our daipers changed and sometimes we cry just to be held. There is no artifice in this, no manipulation; we have a

need and we simply ask for it to be met in the most direct way, in a way that our carers simply cannot ignore.

Little children don't cope easily with change; they thrive on routine. And yet it is during these early years that they begin to face change and the things that may upset their feelings of security: the birth of a sibling, accidents potty training, feeding themselves, starting school. Nothing compares with the learning acquired during the first four years. When we learn to talk we also learn to express needs without crying. Energy is high, and the small child is extremely physical.

Physical connections

Muladhara chakra rules the legs, feet and all solid body parts, including the spine, bones, teeth and nails. It also rules the anus, rectum, colon and prostate, blood and the building of cells. It also relates to the most primitive, reptilian, part of the brain.

Legs play a large part in a child's physical development in the first seven years of life, learning to take the body weight, to walk and to run. The small child learns to

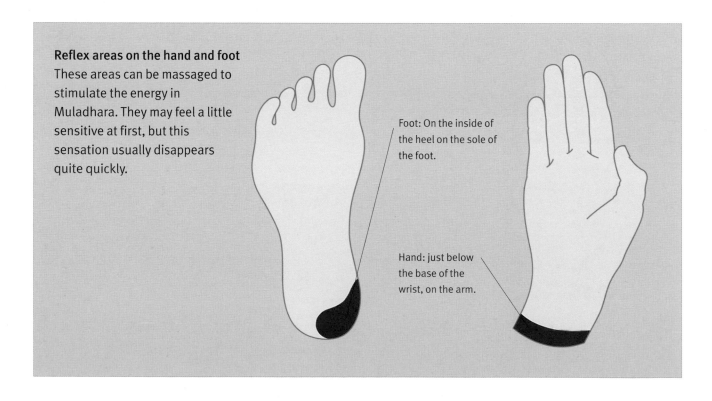

Reflex areas on the hand and foot
These areas can be massaged to stimulate the energy in Muladhara. They may feel a little sensitive at first, but this sensation usually disappears quite quickly.

Foot: On the inside of the heel on the sole of the foot.

Hand: just below the base of the wrist, on the arm.

control elimination. Their first and second teeth are formed during the period. With the right support at this age, a person grows up strong, with straight legs, shiny nails, able to eliminate waste regularly, with healthy circulation and erect stance with a sense of connection to the ground.

If there is weak or blocked energy in Muladhara, there might be problems in any one of the above. The nails may be brittle and there may be problems with the hips and legs and with the bones generally, as well as with the teeth. There may be problems with constipation, ulcerative colitis, piles, prostate cancer, with circulation or various blood diseases, obesity and lack of vitality.

Glands

The governing glands are the adrenals. When we get a fright it is adrenaline that powers our muscles to take action, either by running away or by fighting—the "fight-or-flight" response. The startled deer defecates as it bounds off away from danger: people, too, commonly feel a reaction in the bowels when they experience fear. Unfortunately, in today's high-pressured world, the fight-or-flight response is elicited far more often than is healthy, and there is usually little opportunity to use up the extra adrenaline coursing through the bloodstream as a result. Smokers, far from calming themselves with a cigarette, flood their bloodstream with adrenaline. The result of all this superfluous adrenaline is high blood pressure and a nervous disposition.

The kidney meridian governs our ability to express fear. The crescent-shaped adrenal glands sit right on top of the kidneys, and are influenced by energy in Muladhara and by an excess of fear.

Sound

We connect at Muladhara with our most primal energy, and, accordingly, the music that activates this chakra is tribal and primitive: drums, repetitive rhythms, low tones. Instruments such as the kettle drum, bassoon and double bass, thunderclaps, the rumble of an earthquake, spewing lava pouring down a volcano cracking as it cools, the low rumble of a dog about to snap, the roar of a lion

or the trumpeting of a startled elephant take the energy right down to Muladhara. (I once went to a concert of Japanese Kodo drumming, where the largest drum took several men to move, and supreme strength to play. And when that drum sounded I could feel the vibrations in the base chakra.)

Vowel

Uh, pronounced like the "o" in rope, or "u" in cup, is the vowel tone for Muladhara, and is believed by some to be a harmonic of the frequency of the Earth itself.

Mantra

The sacred bija (seed) mantra to activate Muladhara is Lam (pronounced "lang"). This can be chanted before meditation, and is especially effective when done in one of the sitting postures. You can also repeat the mantra several times with a breath as you do the appropriate postures (see pages 98–100).

Make your lips into a square shape, push your tongue into a square shape also against the soft palate, and make the sound in a gentle, relaxed voice without straining the throat. This will vibrate the palate, brain and top of your cranium, thus preventing the downward movement of energy in the nadis, forcing it upward at the "ang" part of the sound.

Gemstones

Agate, hematite, bloodstone, garnet, red coral, ruby, smoky quartz, tigereye all activate Muladhara. While these gems are believed to energize Muladhara, I don't think you should be too dogmatic when you choose one to suit. If you see or hold another gem that seems to ground you, by all means use that.

Place a stone near the perineum when you are in a sitting posture or when lying down, or hold one or place one nearby when you meditate.

Aromatherapy oils

Cypress, myrrh, patchouli, musk, cedarwood and lavender all activate Muladhara. Put drops in a bath or use a burner, letting your intuition help you choose from the above oils the one/s that make you feel earthed. Add a few drops to a base oil, such as almond, and use it on your legs, buttocks and lower abdomen, or, because smell is especially associated with Muladhara, dab a little just under your nose.

The meridians that control fear have the least energy in the small hours, between 3 and 7 a.m., so it may help to put a few drops on a pillow or a handkerchief at night and keep that near you.

Foods

Root vegetables, spices, onions, garlic and licorice activate Muladhara. Licorice is a bit of a specialist plant, requiring a massive 6 feet (1.8 m) of topsoil to grow. It probes deep into the soil to absorb the nutrients there, and it has a strong effect on the bowels. Root vegetables are known to have a tamasic quality, tending to slow you down, so you might want to watch how much of them you eat if you are already lethargic.

Balanced energy

When the energy in Muladhara is balanced we feel secure, loved, supported by the soil and comfortable in our families. There is a deep connection with the Earth and appreciation for nature and attunement with its cycles. It is easy to achieve goals, and there is primordial trust: there is a belief in the world as a secure and supportive place, a sense of gratitude for Earth's gifts and optimism about its bounty; we are comfortable with our physical bodies and enjoy movement.

Unbalanced or blocked energy

On the physical level there may be bowel problems, such as constipation, diarrhea, irritable bowel syndrome and so on (see Physical connections, page 28–9). There may be tremors, foot problems, insecurity with contact with the ground. Some may break bones or have skeletal problems such as scoliosis or lordosis. Circulation may be problematic, causing symptoms such as high blood pressure, hemorrhoids, Raynaud's syndrome and so on. There may also be lethargy.

On the emotional side, the world is seen as a fearful place, and the perception is that people are out to do you harm. The ground does not feel supportive. Attention revolves primarily around self-indulgences, such as money and possessions and the fear of losing them. It may be difficult to be generous or to receive. Some people with blocked or unbalanced energy here become unstable, inconsistent, jumpy and undependable. There can also be an obsession with dirt and germs. Emotions may swing between being very sweet and vicious cruelty, to the point of self-harm or injury to others. Unbalanced or blocked energy here can also manifest in excessive risk-taking behavior.

Suggestions for balancing Muladhara

- Get your hands in the soil, even if it's only growing a potted plant.
- Wear red, especially red underpants.
- Hold one of the associated gemstones, or put it on your body near the root chakra.
- Repeat the mantra *Lam*.
- Play tribal music, take up drumming, stamp your feet.
- Walk barefoot on the grass or beach.
- Sing *Uh* (in the key of lower C).
- Sit and watch sunrise or sunset, aware of your tailbone touching the ground.
- Hug a tree.
- Before each meal, silently give thanks to Mother Nature for sustaining you.
- Use your sense of smell consciously to sharpen it.
- Fragrance your room/clothes with the associated oils.
- Stay inside—hole up indoors.
- Cook yourself nutritious, wholesome food, especially root vegetables.
- Fix your roof or anything else about your house that makes you feel insecure.
- When you feel the spontaneous instinct to give, follow it.
- Spend time outdoors in natural surroundings.
- Choose one of the deities and study the associated mythology.
- Do the yoga postures on pages 98–100.
- Practice pranayama regularly, shown on pages 137–43.
- Try the visualization on page 152.

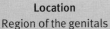

svadisthana gateway of the moon

SVA = THAT WHICH IS ITSELF *DHISTHANA* = ONE'S OWN ABODE, HOME OF THE SELF OR SWEETNESS

Location

The location of the Svadisthana chakra is in the region of the genitals. More precisely, the chakra can be seen spinning counter-clockwise in men, clockwise in women, in the lower abdomen near the genitals/ovaries and womb, but it originates nearer the sacrum or the tip of the coccyx, and projects backward from there as well. Interestingly, the word *sacrum* comes from the Latin, meaning "sacred bone," and is believed to be the site of the soul. The difference between where it is seen on the outer body and its origination sometimes gives rise to confusion about its location. With the source being so close to the root chakra, Muladhara, there are some similar functions. Svadisthana is also associated with the extra chakra known as the Tan Tien (pronounced dan dien), which is about four fingers width below the navel.

Purpose

The purpose of this chakra is to generate creativity, sexuality and pleasure. As the alternative translation of *dhisthana* is "sweetness," this perhaps gives the best clue as to the energy of this chakra. More than just sexual pleasure, I am talking about the sweet delight of waking up each morning optimistic, confident and full of enthusiasm for what the day may bring. Svadisthana holds this potential.

This fecund chakra is responsible not only for the conception, gestation and birth of babies—ideas form in a similar way. There are opportunities for creativity at any given moment, and with Svadisthana well balanced, we will see them come to fruition.

There is a special connection between this chakra and the fifth chakra, Vishuddha, which also relates to creativity. At this level, however, the vibrations are lower and the creativity more personal. But just imagine the boost given to creativity when it connects to the transpersonal in the throat chakra.

Second of the three personal chakras, Svadisthana provides a still point where creativity may flower. The French word for pelvis is basin, and the pelvis is indeed like a type of basin or pool. (We talk of pooling ideas; the element of this chakra is water.) I think of Svadisthana cradling the sacred energy of creativity, brimming over with ideas and enthusiasm, not to mention sexual energy. It is a place of play between the grounding, supportive and structuring energy of Muladhara, and the more outgoing chakra of personal power, Manipura, at the solar plexus.

Many people find the answer to the question "who am I?" when they get in touch with their creativity. Night schools are full of enthusiastic adults taking their life into new areas, and surprising themselves with formerly hidden talents. All of us could benefit from letting our life choices be made from this source of creativity and inner wisdom. Subconsciously we usually know

the right choices to make regarding our happiness. But intuition is more often than not inconvenient; it tells us to ditch the boring office job and go and help orphans in some distant land, which is a scary thought. However, we ignore it at the cost of energy balance in Svadisthana.

Sexual energy is the driving force behind so many human achievements; it is hard to know where to begin when describing its importance as part of our energy system. The human sex drive is present throughout the year, at all times. The sexual union of a man and woman when performed out of love and respect can be a truly transcendent act, with power not only to bond the couple, but to grow their love out into the world toward all sentient beings.

True sexual love is generous and accepting, and pays more attention to inner beauty than outer form. When we see ourselves in symbolic union with another, and as part of the cosmic force of the multiverse, it helps us to accommodate differences.

The physical act of sexual intercourse strongly unites the first two chakras of the couple, and has the potential to raise the Kundalini energy through the other chakras (see page 18). Orgasm is perhaps the closest most people come to experiencing spiritual bliss. Sexual energy is controlled in Tantric sex practices to divert the power of the orgasm up the chakras to the crown, rather than discharge it locally in the genitals. Tantric statues of gods and goddesses making love actually represent unity of wisdom and compassion. There is an aura about a couple who have recently made love in its purest form; it is a most healing thing, not just for the couple but for the people around them.

Svadisthana plays a crucial role in relationships, and relationships are our teachers. Remember that when you point a finger at someone else, three fingers point back at you. Uncomfortable though it may be to admit, more often than not the things that drive us mad about another person are aspects of ourselves that we are keeping well repressed. We attract people to ourselves to learn specific lessons: relationships expose both our strengths and our weaknesses, our strongly held beliefs and how we wish to be.

There is another association with this chakra: money. Do we utilize our talents creatively to support ourselves, or have we prostituted ourselves in order to put bread on the table? Do we wear the golden handcuffs of a mortgage paid, at the cost of creativity stifled? The colon is ruled by Svadisthana and, as I describe in the section on Physical connections on page 36–7, there is a definite link between finances and the element of the colon meridian: metal. Self-worth is often mistakenly confused with accumulation of money.

Color

Svadisthana radiates a vibrant orange, almost gold at times, and it stimulates movement, enhances dance and promotes joyfulness, light release and pleasure. Blind people feel color. Orange has vibrations that resonate within an octave of our own DNA molecules. The word *orange* comes from the Arabic, *nananj*, meaning orange fruit, and also refers to the pomegranate, which has orange seeds—a well-known aphrodisiac and thought also to bring joy and relief from depression. No wonder the lamas and monks I met in Nepal and Laos, who spend their lives in orange robes, are such radiant, joyful people. People with vibrant energy in Svadisthana seem to bring an element of creativity into whatever they do; the true Midas touch.

Element

The element associated with this chakra is water. Take a moment to jot down words you associate with water. The chances are that apart from names for its form, such as river, snow, steam, ice, rain, lake, sea and so on, you also have words for its habits: flowing, raging, trickle, torrent and so on. Maybe you have some words that

relate to what it can do: fertilize, quench, grow, cleanse. There may be some negative words: drought, tsunami, blocked and polluted. Are you beginning to see the extent of the influence of water on life? We should never underestimate the power of water. Like the surface of our planet, our bodies are made up of 70 percent water. The tides can be measured in the fluids of our bodies.

In Chinese medicine, the kidneys and bladder are governed by the water element, which in turn rules fear. We fear loss of control, or control by others, or failing health. There is often a primal fear of abandonment (especially strong as we enter into new and intimate relationships). Money issues can make us fearful, as can betrayal. In the end we have to accept that events are ultimately out of our control, and our lives are more effective when we learn to go with the flow, trusting to a greater power. We need to allow the free flow of emotions. Creative energy breaks us out of our habitual patterns of behavior, our ruts; it is at odds with repetition. Next time you go to a familiar beach, look at how the tidal flow changes the size and shape of the rock pools and sandbanks. We need to develop the same flexibility; Svadisthana can help us.

Sense

This chakra governs our ability to taste. If I ask you to think of your favorite fruit, sun ripened, cut into sections, dripping juice, smelling fragrant, the odds are that your mouth will start to water. When the element of water is linked with the sense of taste, many flavors are revealed. So often we down our food and don't bother to really taste it. It benefits Svadisthana to eat more consciously, savoring every mouthful and chewing it slowly. Svadisthana helps us to taste the sweetness of life, guilt free and with enthusiasm, and this may require us to slow down generally.

Age

Svadisthana is strongest between the ages of 7 and 14 years. Children in this age range have already faced the first rite of passage: starting school. Their world has, therefore, already opened out significantly and they are

The symbol of Svadisthana

The six-petalled lotus of Svadisthana is colored vermilion in ancient texts and marked with Sanskrit letters. The color of this chakra's symbol indicates the strong influence that impulses, ideas and desires have on the mind. A sexual relationship can provide a wellspring of creativity.

The yantra is a crescent moon. The center of the symbol is often colored a light gray or green, like the sea. Within the crescent moon is a mythical creature called a makara—a fish-tailed alligator. (Jung called this the Leviathan of the waters, implying an enormous whale-like creature.)

Deities—Vishnu and Rakini

It is traditional for each chakra to have a representation of a divine pair within its symbol.

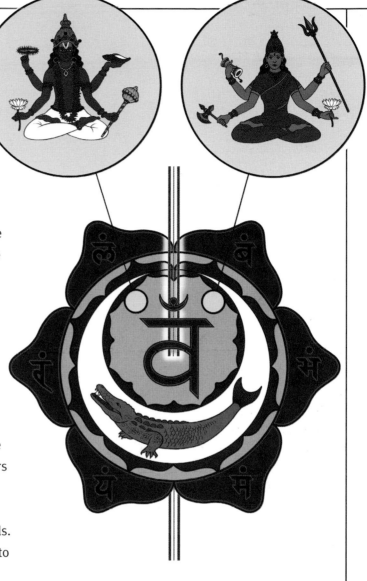

Vishnu, the supreme, or original, solar god, can take many forms. He has striking dark blue skin and wears a garland of forest flowers, a vanamala, around his neck. In one hand he holds a conch shell. This is to remind us that we need to develop our listening skills. He holds a disc in another hand, indicating the need to concentrate in order to hit a target. The mace or war club in another hand tells us of the fight we all have to undertake to subdue our ego. And, finally, the lotus blossom reminds us of our spiritual goal in life.

Rakini, the goddess of this chakra, is an aspect of Sarasvati, wife of Brahma, who is associated with flowing speech. She carries a Neptune-like trident, here representing the essential unity of body, mind and spirit. She beats out a rhythm with a drum, and holds a lotus flower reminding us that victory is possible for anyone. The battle-ax she carries in another hand speaks of the aspirant's struggle to overcome negative attributes. Often shown with a fierce face and protruding teeth, she reminds us of the dangers of an untrained imagination.

exposed to the "law of the playground," not to mention all the varying family ethics of their schoolmates. Out of this melee of ideas and influences they start to work out what matters to them.

Svadisthana governs morality, our personal code of behavior, as opposed to Muladhara, which governs the law of the tribe. It could be called the chakra of ethics, where we learn to honor one another. The first step on the eightfold path (see page 21) is the so-called yamas: a commitment to nonviolence, truthfulness, honesty, self-restraint and sharing—lessons we learn in the playground and from teachers in an ideal world, even if we have not learned them at home. We also learn to be loyal to our friends, and to be quiet and to listen— to allow other flowering personalities space. Given the right circumstances, children at this age are mostly very sweet, creative, enthusiastic and curious, and with a natural compassion for others.

It is during this age that sexuality begins to flower— much sooner than most parents like to acknowledge. Young girls in the West today often start to menstruate at nine years of age. Children this age need help learning how to handle strong feelings. The school curriculum should allow sufficient space for creativity to develop and where emotions may be expressed, and Svadisthana helps these to flower.

Physical connections

Svadisthana governs the pelvis, reproductive organs, womb, kidney, bladder and colon and lower back, as well as fluids such as blood, sperm, lymph and gastric juices.

Reproduction is affected by the energy in this chakra, and treating the kidney energy is often the first step acupuncturists take when trying to correct infertility.

I have already mentioned that the water element rules the kidneys and bladder, and our ability to express fear appropriately. Between the ages of 7 and 14 should be the time when confidence develops, and fear is appropriate and protective. We all need a healthy measure of fear in our lives; what we don't need is for it to rule our lives.

The colon meridian, in the metal element, has the psychological function of helping us to express grief

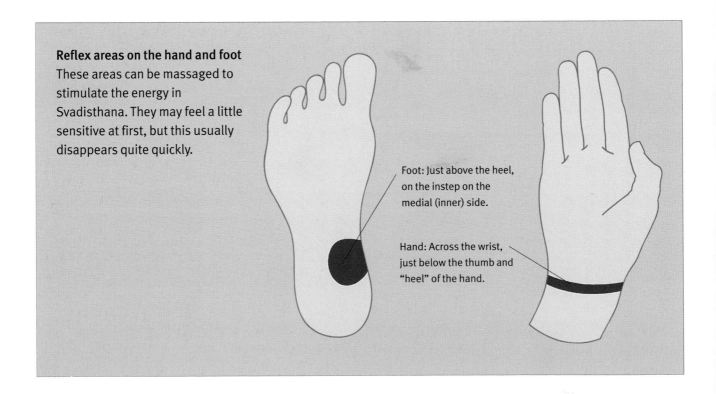

Reflex areas on the hand and foot
These areas can be massaged to stimulate the energy in Svadisthana. They may feel a little sensitive at first, but this usually disappears quite quickly.

Foot: Just above the heel, on the instep on the medial (inner) side.

Hand: Across the wrist, just below the thumb and "heel" of the hand.

appropriately. Physically, it eliminates waste from the body; psychologically, it helps rid us of regrets, grief and toxic negativity, which crush confidence and stifle creativity.

There can be all sorts of physical problems associated with malfunctioning energy in Svadisthana: kidney and bladder problems, infertility, impotence, cancers of the womb, ovaries and prostate, blood diseases, low sperm count and problems with lymph and gastric juices.

Glands

The governing glands in Svadisthana are the ovaries, testicles and prostate. Although it is sometimes said that the brain is the largest sex organ in the body, these glands play a principal role in sexual creativity.

Sound

Flowing music, belly-dance music, dancing couples, folk music and salsa are associated with this chakra. In nature, it is birdsong, flowing water and fountains.

Any music/dance that gets your pelvis moving benefits Svadisthana. It is an area often held rigid, especially in cold climates. A prudish attitude to moving the hips and pelvis does us no favors at all—it seems that Elvis Presley had the right idea! In Egypt, belly dance is used by women to help them prepare for childbirth. The movements described in Chapter Four (see page 95) help to free up this area.

Vowel

O, as in the word November, sung in the key of D, is the vowel tone for Svadisthana. Intone the note gently, using it like a mantra, or repeat it as you do the postures for Svadisthana (see pages 101–5). Because of the connection between Svadisthana and Vishudda, the throat chakra, using the voice is particularly potent.

Mantra

Pronounced "vang," Vam is the sacred bija (seed) mantra for Svadisthana and will free blocked energy in this area. Concentrate on Svadisthana while you chant it. This doesn't need to be done very loudly, just allow a natural resonance to build.

Gemstones

Carnelian, moonstone, citrine, tourmaline and golden topaz all increase energy in Svadisthana. However, as before, if you feel drawn to a particular stone that you sense stimulates your creativity, then use that. Lying down, place your chosen stone or stones on your lower abdomen and visualize absorbing the vibrations.

Aromatherapy oils

Ylang-ylang, sandalwood, jasmine, rose and petigrain stimulate Svadisthana. Use a few drops of one or more, chosen intuitively—by sniffing them and seeing which oil attracts you—in your bath, or in a burner. Blend a few drops in base oil, such as almond, and massage your lower abdomen and throat with it. Better still, since this is the chakra of sexuality and creativity, why not use them to share a massage with your partner, surrounded by a large circle of orange candles. If you have an orange sarong, towel or piece of fabric, use this to cover the parts that are not being massaged. Turn off the lights and enjoy releasing the exquisite energy of Svadisthana.

Foods

Leafy vegetables, salad greens, watercress, cucumber, melon, pears and quince activate Svadisthana. Most of the foods that stimulate this chakra are high in water content. Quinces and pomegranates are thought by some to be aphrodisiacs.

Balanced energy

Children with balanced energy in Svadisthana epitomize the sovereign child: full of innocent wonder and delight in the world, with an enthusiasm for life and appreciation of its beauty.

Adults with balanced energy in Svadisthana chakra are creative and inspiring people to be around. They are confident, open, friendly and express a deep joy in life that is wonderfully infectious. They express their sexuality with naturalness, without guilt, and form appropriate relationships. They are accepting of their bodies, feel good in their skins, and generally have a confident self-image. Not burdened with an oversized ego or feelings of low self-worth, they have a balanced and harmonious aura about them. They also have healthy reproductive organs and a strongly integrated creative life. Their attitude to their finances is balanced and generous. Feelings are accepted and expressed with a flow. They are considerate to others, while at the same time honoring their own feelings.

Unbalanced or blocked energy

When there is blocked energy here in Svadisthana, sexual expression may, as a result, be inhibited, inappropriate or misdirected. There may also be excessive fantasies, coarse sexuality, coldness or emotional paralysis. A person with malfunctioning energy in Svadisthana is not able to take life's knocks and see the bigger picture. We are likely to see an isolated martyr, a person who is uncertain and full of mistrust in the world, with a pessimistic outlook —in the extreme, perhaps even a pedophile.

Physically there may be sexual difficulties, such as impotence/frigidity, kidney or bladder problems and low back pain, fibroids, ovarian cysts and prostate problems. It is worth noting here that Chinese medicine teaches us that we are born with a certain amount of original chi, which is expendable throughout our life. We also receive chi/prana from food, pure air, water, good company and so on, but this original chi is finite—and men lose a little bit of it every time they orgasm. Too much sex depletes this original chi to the detriment of health. How much is too much you may ask. If you feel regularly exhausted after sex, you might want to conserve your energy in this arena. Certainly Svadisthana energy is compromised by careless sex—note, I do not say carefree. This is a most sacred part of our body and our being, and we need to honor how we use it.

Low back problems, prostate cancer and so on are often linked to sudden financial loss, as are bowel cancer and bowel problems generally. The metal element refers to the precious minerals in the rocks, and it connects with our relationship we have with our fathers, and the heavenly father—in other words, our spirituality. It governs our feelings of self-worth and spiritual attunement. People with an imbalance in Svadisthana often feel worthless, lack spiritual connection and overcompensate by accumulating money. Its loss, therefore, can be a devastating event.

Suggestions for balancing Svadisthana

- Keep a journal and record your feelings first thing each morning.
- Reflect on what sex means to you, and how you express it.
- Look at how you express your male/female sides, and think about how you might do this more creatively.
- Take time with the sensual side of sex, rather than racing to orgasm.
- Learn to belly dance/dance in couples/salsa.
- Do the postures for Svadisthana illustrated on pages 101–5.
- Try the visualization on page 153.
- Breathe as if following wave rhythms on a beach.
- Sit by water in the moonlight and look at the reflections.
- Swim breaststroke in the sea and be aware how it opens the pelvis and Svadisthana.
- Analyze your relationship with money and think about how you use it.
- Think of ways to bring creativity into your working life.
- Look at your personal code of ethics. Are you honoring it?
- Do you honor yourself and others in relationships?
- Use the oils or gemstones suggested in the previous pages.
- Fill a vase with marigolds and light an orange candle.
- Think of someone you admire who expresses enthusiasm and creativity in their life, and try to emulate them.

manipura gateway of the sun

MANIPURA = CITY OF JEWELS

Location

The location of this chakra is in the region of the solar plexus. Manipura energy emanates forward from a level of the spine, between the 12th thoracic vertebra and the 1st lumbar vertebra, expanding approximately to an area covering two finger-widths both above and below the navel. Called the solar plexus chakra, Manipura's position also extends below the solar plexus. Located behind it on the spine is one of the most significant acupuncture points, known as "ming men." It is considered to be the seat of the original chi that forms humans, and while it relates most to Svadisthana (see pages 32–9), it also affects Manipura.

Purpose

The purpose of Manipura is to manifest personal power and self-mastery. Manipura chakra is primarily associated with sight, with fire and with light. To obtain an insight into the energy of this chakra, imagine watching the sun rise. Feel the excitement of expectation as light spreads first across a patch of the sky in the east and then watch as color floods back into the landscape. And then, when the fiery sun crests the horizon, there is an immediate sensation of warmth. The dawn chorus reaches a crescendo, flowers open and turn to face the sun and another day begins, full of possibilities.

The golden symbol of Manipura chakra (see pages 42–3) can be interpreted as representing the surface of the planet, heaven above, earth below. Manipura energy emanating radiant yellow/gold light is the sunrise on our horizon, enabling us to shine our light on the world. Energy found here determines how we feel at the start of the day—whether we wake up and are full of optimism and enthusiasm or wish that we could dive back under the covers and hope for it all to go away.

The way in which we express personal power—with strength and confidence, energy and enthusiasm on the one hand, or by being tyrannical and domineering or a victim of circumstance on the other —is governed by the balance of energy in Manipura chakra. Our very social identity is forged in the fire of this chakra: when energy concentrates in Manipura, we receive help in establishing our place on the Earth. In Manipura we have the potential to evolve a more enlightened perspective of love and truth on the world.

In his yoga sutras, in which Patanjali (see page 21) provides the moral and physical framework for achieving absolute freedom of the self, says that the contemplation of Manipura leads to knowledge of the physical organism and its functions, and that this is the chakra of the life force. This aligns with the energy of two important acupuncture points: "exhausted spirit," found in the navel; and "destiny gate/gate of life," situated between the 2nd and 3rd lumbar vertebrae.

Color

The color projecting forward from Manipura is yellow ranging to gold. Its direction of spin is clockwise in men (viewed from the front), and counterclockwise in women. You can stimulate Manipura by wearing a yellow/gold belt, or a scarf around your waist, or by wearing a yellow vest or dressing in yellow more generally. Surrounding yourself with vibrant yellow objects—candles, cushions or fabrics, for example—also stimulates Manipura. Yellow is a highly visible color, known to be confidence-inspiring. It is used extensively when people, or vehicles for that matter, need to be noticed: for safety clothing, for rescue vehicles and, of course, for school buses.

Age

Although Manipura is strongest between the ages of 14 and 21, it is when we go through the "terrible 2s" that we test out the energy of this chakra for the first time, seeing how far we can go expressing our will until our parents snap. But it is during the mid to late teens that the flames in the belly are well and truly fanned (as parents of recalcitrant teenagers will testify). At this time, the need to express individuality rightly becomes strongly evident. Hopefully there are circumstances that allow for this flowering, encouraging individuals to discover their strengths and how they might use these to serve society and gain acceptance. In most societies, there are rituals for attaining manhood/womanhood, be it the traditional trade apprentice system, the high school prom dance on graduation, the start of menstruation, shaving or killing your first pig in the forest.

The consequences of limiting the expression of Manipura energy at this time may be dire—the energy will come out, but in some distorted form: fans fighting at soccer matches, spraying graffiti on buildings and road bridges, showing off, potentially lethally, in cars or on motorbikes. It is no surprise to me that some of the most destructive computer hackers, people who spend hours in their bedrooms late at night maliciously devising bugs to mess with the Internet, turn out to be teenage boys. It is so much harder in an expanding population to make your mark than it is in tight-knit communities where the elders are role models and mentors for the young.

The archetype of Manipura is the spiritual warrior, setting forth with courage into the wider world to seek fame and fortune; as opposed to the drudge, daunted by such a journey, who is defeated by a challenge before it even begins.

Element

Without the rising sun there would be no life on Earth, or humans to set a fire, the element of this chakra. When the molten fiery energy from the center of our Earth breaks the surface, and becomes visible in a volcano, we experience its power. Standing near the cinder fields of Mount Merapi in Java, I heard the volcano cracking and rumbling long before I saw it spewing out golden magma, lighting up the night sky. It was an awesome, captivating sight, one that called me closer. Fire always attracts people, drawing human beings together. Good leaders, such as Nelson Mandela, attract enormous crowds of people with the magnetism they project. But we need to use power appropriately for the greater betterment of humanity (after all, Adolf Hitler also drew huge numbers of people) by developing evolved power in this chakra.

Fire cleans and purifies, it warms our bodies as well as our food. Heat is generated when we transmute the food in our bellies into the fuel needed to run our bodily

The symbol of Manipura

Traditionally, the ten-petalled lotus blossom that symbolizes Manipura is colored a greenish-blue, like a rain cloud, each petal inscribed with a Sanskrit letter in bright blue. Inside the petals is found a circle containing a red downward-pointing triangle with T-shaped projections symbolizing movement. The Sanskrit for the bija mantra, Ram, is found within this, colored red. Located at the bottom of the triangle is a red ram, the vehicle of Agni, the vedic fire god, representing the qualities of Manipura. One way you can stimulate Manipura is to visualize a red triangle while you meditate.

Deities—Lakini, Agni, Kali, Surya and Rudra

The deities that are associated with each of the chakras represent the personal qualities that we can expect to be influenced by the energy emanating from that location. Manipura chakra has four such deities rather than the usual two.

Lakini, a red-colored goddess with four arms, is one. Her teeth protrude and her chest is spattered with blood and fat from her predilection for eating a raw-meat diet. She holds two symbols: a vajra, or thunderbolt, in one hand, and fire in another. The other two hands form the mudras vara (granting benefits) and abhaya with hand facing forward (dispelling fear).

Agni (Apollo), the fire god, protector and guardian of homes, is the god connected with this chakra. Picture a protective fire at the mouth of a cave in order to remember him.

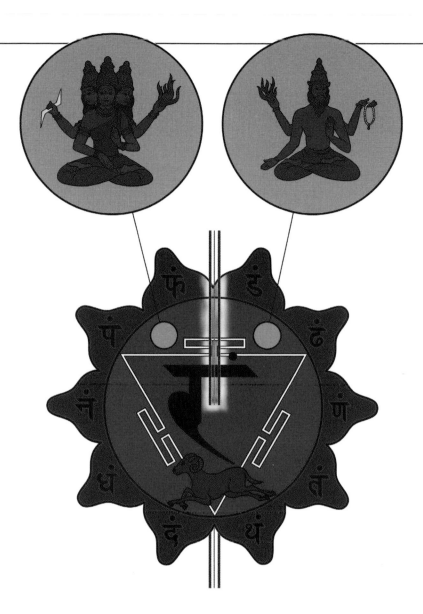

Kali, the black warrior goddess, known for her contrasting ferocious, bloodthirsty nature and her compassion, at the same time has the ability to dispel ignorance.

Surya, the sun god, represents our ability to shine. You may be familiar with surya namaskar, the yoga sequence to greet the sun. It is particularly powerful at energizing all the chakras and is most effective when done at the start of the day. It is interesting to note that of Surya's many names (there are 12 in all) one is Vivasvat—the god of good digestion.

Rudra, the god of fire and storms, is the destructive aspect of Shiva. He also has the ability to bestow blessings in abundance. He reminds us that learning to ride life's storms strengthens us, and is part of maturity.

systems. A good, hot meal nourishes and revives us. Fire kept us warm at night for many eons, and provided our only illumination once the sun had set. Even in today's world, it protects us from wild animals, regenerates our crops and cremates us when we die.

Sense

Bearing in mind that in the absence of sunlight we see almost nothing of our surroundings, it is easy to remember that sight is the sense associated with Manipura chakra. Chinese medicine acknowledges that the liver meridian controls sight and, psychologically, foresight as well. The liver is one of the organs governed by Manipura. To be warriors, to set off into the world and to make our contribution to society, we need not only know what direction to strike out in, but also to be able to predict the consequences of the actions we take.

If the energy in this chakra is disturbed in some way, perhaps by being over- or underactive or by being unbalanced or blocked (see page 46), it can manifest in problems with sight. The eye exercises (see pages 118–19) are beneficial to this chakra in this respect, and work on the levels of both sight and foresight.

Physical connections

Manipura rules the liver, gallbladder, spleen, stomach and kidneys. The digestive system is also influenced by Manipura. As I have already pointed out, sight and foresight are governed by the liver. Its paired wood element meridian, the gallbladder, not only metabolizes fats, it also helps us to make decisions, and together they help us to express anger in an appropriate fashion. When our teenage children seem to swing wildly between anger and frustration and being the calmest, sweetest beings on Earth, they are trying to balance the expression of power here. How we exert our will, getting the balance right between being retiring or overdomineering, is down to the effective functioning of the wood element, and to the smooth flow of Manipura energy.

The stomach and spleen not only assimilate and convert nutrients from the food we ingest, thus providing fuel for our bodies, they also govern our

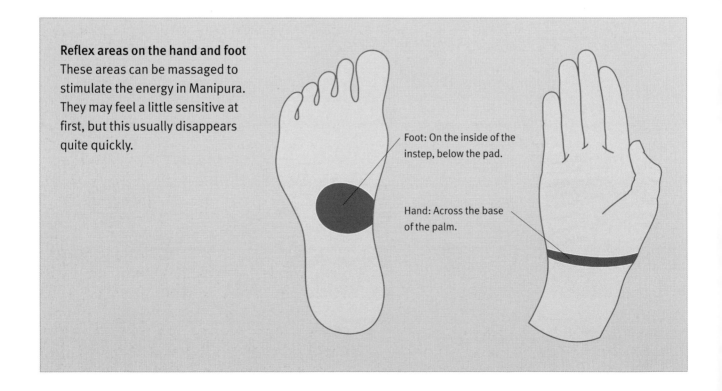

Reflex areas on the hand and foot
These areas can be massaged to stimulate the energy in Manipura. They may feel a little sensitive at first, but this usually disappears quite quickly.

Foot: On the inside of the instep, below the pad.

Hand: Across the base of the palm.

relationship with food. They affect personal power by motivating us into action, and influence our ability to express sympathy appropriately. This is known as the earth element. Unbalanced energy here can lead to negative feelings of martyrdom.

Although they are not traditionally associated with this chakra, I would also include the kidneys here, for they are found in the region, tucked protectively under the lower ribs. Having a strong influence on courage, they must affect the energy in Manipura.

The abdomen, lower back and autonomic nervous system are all influenced by Manipura. The postures suggested for this chakra (see page 106–9) greatly strengthen these areas of the body as well as improve the functioning of the associated organs.

Gland

The governing gland in this chakra is the pancreas. Close to the spleen, it plays a role in digestion.

Sound

Whenever you hear any strong composition of bold, orchestral music, or watch a marching band pass by, the chances are that you will feel a tingle of excitement somewhere in your belly. Music such as this, which is able to fire our beings with enthusiasm, can be used to activate Manipura.

You can also try listening to Tibetan overtone chanting. If you are interested in this type of music, it is possible to learn to perform it on your own, but I recommend joining a workshop to get yourself started. The overtones are very powerful indeed, especially so when they are performed in a group.

Vowel

O, as in the word go, is the vowel sound for the Manipura chakra. Chant this in the key of E.

Mantra

The scared bija (seed) mantra to activate Manipura is Ram—easy to remember as the animal for this chakra is the fiery-natured ram. Chant the mantra while sitting in a comfortable meditation pose, or repeat it while you perform the postures recommend for Manipura (see page 106–9), apart from the abdominal lift.

Gemstones

Amber, tigereye, yellow citrine and topaz, agate, aventurine and sunstone all activate Manipura. As suggested previously, chose your stone or stones intuitively from those above that make you feel strong and confident. Place them around you on your desk, or altar, or lie down and place them on your belly, where there is a convenient little hollow to hold them. Amber is a particularly good choice, feeling warm to the touch, and it is highly beneficial for the endocrine system and the spleen, as well as heart. Tigereye helps us to feel brave, like a tiger, while citrine raises our self-esteem.

Aromatherapy oils

Bergamot, ylang-ylang, cinnamon, chamomile, lemon, thyme and vetiver all help to activate this chakra. Put a few drops in a burner, or massage a mix of oils of your choice from those noted above in a base oil, such as almond, into your abdomen.
Caution: A word of warning—never go out in the sunshine with neat bergamot on your skin as it may react with the ultraviolet content of the light.

Foods

The liver, gallbladder, spleen and stomach meridians are all in the domain of Manipura chakra, and digestion in general is ruled by this chakra. We can eat foods that support these meridians if we feel we have problems in Manipura. Sour foods and grains activate Manipura. Sour foods support the liver and gallbladder. Citrus fruits are good and quince is exceptional. Grains and simple foods, such as muesli, whole-wheat bread, rice and so on, support the stomach and spleen. Try muesli with fresh orange juice with a quince grated into it.

Many people manifest an imbalance in this chakra with digestive problems. It is common for small children who are feeling unconfident at school to complain of a tummy ache, or go off their food, or certain foods. We have learned over the years to override vital information from our stomachs about when we have had enough food. How many times were you told as a child to "clean your plate"? And sometimes we are so busy we forget to eat, ignoring hunger messages. Many of us need to examine our relationship to food, and relearn how to listen to the messages from our stomach, examine our eating habits and learn to notice how they reflect our emotions. Because this chakra is highly relevant to all digestive problems, the foods we are drawn to, or have distaste for, can give us many clues about its state of health. We can reflect on how we express ourselves and our state of confidence.

Balanced energy

When the energy in this chakra is balanced we are strong, confident and certain of our place in the world. As a result, we do not need to be overassertive in order to get our way or achieve our goal; we already command respect from others and give it in equal measure. Our opinions, individuality and calm strength earn us this respect. We are motivated to work for the general good of those around us and the wider society. We are warriors, able to face the challenges that are set before us each day with determination and optimism. As a consequence of a well-rounded personality, feelings are recognized, not denied, and they are expressed in an appropriate fashion.

If the Sushumna (see pages 16–17) makes a strong connection between this chakra, the third eye (Ajna) and the crown (Sahasara) chakras, then your innermost desires may be achieved. Named the "city of jewels," Manipura is said to bestow the ability to find hidden treasure on those whose energy is free-flowing and balanced here. This I would normally interpret as spiritual treasure, but I have also known it to happen quite literally on the material level.

A person with balanced energy in Manipura will look toned and strong in the midriff. Their abdomen will not protrude, or cave in, and they will have good digestion, and are able to transform what they eat into healthy energy. They are likely to make good choices about what they eat, and stop when they feel satiated. There is a calmness and an inner strength to people who are balanced in Manipura, an equilibrium between the spiritual and the material providing a sense of poise and stability.

Unbalanced or blocked energy

Physically there may be digestive problems—including such ailments as diabetes, ulcers, bulimia, anorexia, excessive eating, bloated stomach, gallstones, liver or eye problems—when there is unbalanced or blocked energy in Manipura. There may also be problems along the pathways of the liver, gallbladder, stomach and spleen, and kidneys meridians. Research has shown that having excess body fat in this area particularly is dangerous for the heart.

If the energy is blocked or excessive in Manipura, the person affected may be domineering, aggressive, pushy and inconsiderate of others. Depending on personality, they may also be workaholics, materialistic, angry, controlling, vain or proud.

If the energy is blocked or weak in Manipura, they may fear being alone, be insecure and need constant reassurance. They may lack confidence, be meek and submissive and unable to stand up for themselves. Easily discouraged, life appears full of obstacles to them—their lack of fire and enthusiasm is palpable.

People with this temperament often show it in having a hollow, rather caved-in belly. To an observer, they may look as if they can't take the "punches" that life throws at them, and a block at this chakra prevents the opening of the higher chakras.

Suggestions for balancing Manipura

- Chant the mantra *Ram*, or the vowel sound *O* in the key of E.
- Wear yellow/gold, especially around the waist.
- Meditate on the chakra's symbol, or on a red triangle.
- Contemplate the hidden meaning in the deities.
- Play bold orchestral or marching music.
- Eat sour foods or grains.
- Use the associated oils to massage your belly, or to fragrance your room.
- Place one of the associated gemstones on your belly.
- Watch a sunrise, gaze at a candle flame or sit by an open fire.
- Close your eyes and feel the sunshine on them.
- Perform the yoga postures suggested on pages 106–9.
- Do the visualization suggested on page 153.
- Try the bellows breath shown on page 140.
- Take time to reflect on how you use power.
- Acknowledge your achievements realistically.
- Keep a journal and record your feelings.
- Think about how anger plays out in your life.
- Do something new that stretches you beyond your usual comfort zone.
- Finish a meal feeling you could eat a little more.
- Learn to listen to the messages from your stomach.
- Keep this area warm and don't expose it to cold wind.
- Visualize a corset of strength around your middle when you are scared.
- Make regular checks on your posture to draw your tummy in, or align the pelvis.
- Take time to reflect on your relationship with food.

anahata gateway of the winds

ANAHATA = THE UNSTRUCK SOUND

Location
The middle of the chest or between the breasts

Purpose
Compassion, unconditional love, empathy

Color
Green

Element
Air

Symbol
12-petalled lotus

Age
21–28 years of age

Mantra
Yam

Vowel
Ah, as in scarf

Balanced energy
Compassionate
Unconditional love
Empathetic
Truthful
Receptive
Responsible
Vocational
Altruistic
Generous
Sensitive
Radiating warmth

Unbalanced or blocked energy
Uncaring
Unfeeling
Abuse of love
Abuse of alcohol/drugs
Unforgiving
Angry
Hateful
Needy
Selfish
Jealous
Confused

Location

It is significant that Anahata projects forward between the breasts, in the center of the chest, from its inception at a level on the spine between the 4th and 5th thoracic vertebrae, for this chakra relates strongly to how we nurture others as well as ourselves. We automatically place a hand on that part of the body where it projects backward when we comfort a friend. In the region of the lungs, it governs inspiration on all levels of the body/mind/spirit.

Purpose

The purpose of Anahata is compassion and unconditional love and empathy. At Anahata there is a transition from the more personal functions of the lower three chakras, our foundations, to the interpersonal. The profound lesson Anahata teaches is that true transformation requires us to move beyond the ego, to express divine/unconditional Love. This is called bhakti yoga.

If you picture a person standing with arms outstretched you will see that Anahata sits at the center of a cross. Here, the right and left polarities of the body, represented by right and left arms, meet the rising female/yin energies from the Earth and the descending male/yang energies from the heavens. Below are the chakras of personal survival, biological self-maintenance: self-preservation, sex and food. Above are the three chakras of a more evolved, transpersonal consciousness.

The heart meridian travels down the inside of the arms to the little finger tip—appropriately ending in the hands, for Anahata governs our ability to be touched, to be inspired. A person with an open, unblocked heart chakra is affected by people, events, music and an inspiring landscape. You feel compassion and may be moved to tears. Our language is full of references to this ability: something is deeply heartfelt; we are heartsick with depression or despair; our hearts go out to somebody in distress; we feel heartache; or we suffer from a broken heart. The whole world was touched when a tsunami took the lives of approximately 300,000 people on December 26, 2004, and destroyed the homes and livelihoods of millions more. The upwelling of love and compassion that followed as the rest of the world responded was unprecedented, and every bit as powerful as the original wave.

It is relatively easy to feel energy in this chakra. There is an unmistakable physical sensation in the heart when it activates strongly, allowing even the most armored of people to feel compassion. The emotion inspires us to act to help or comfort others, literally reaching out to them. It is here that the second knot, the vishnu granthi (see page 20), resides. When this unties, we open to new realities, limited views or prejudices are dissolved and there is a flow of unconditional love. Ramakrishna, a fully

enlightened being who experienced the complete rising of Kundalini (see page 18), said that releasing the block at this stage allows us to see the beauty and glory of divine light, and consequently the mind no longer runs after worldly pleasures. As Anahata opens, the brow chakra, Ajna, also begins to open, making us even more receptive to subtler dimensions.

Situated close by Anahata, and paired with it, is one of the minor chakras, Kalpavriksha (the wish-fulfilling kalpa tree). Described in detail in the next chapter (see page 84), Kalpavriksha opens only when Anahata has already done so.

As I mentioned in the last section, on Manipura chakra (see pages 40–7), the diaphragm is seen in many cultures as being like the surface of the Earth. Here, then, we are in the heavens, where the sun shines in its full glory, inspiring the human spirit and radiating warmth (the heart meridian peaks in energy for two hours from around 11 a.m. until 1 p.m.). The diaphragm is connected to the heart via the pericardium, which sheaths it, and this means that each time we breathe we gently massage the heart.

It is often said that in order to love others, we must first learn to love ourselves. Joyless people who are full of self-loathing need to overcome this before they can truly open their heart to others. The Tibetan lamas who taught me often commented on the low self-esteem of people in the West, amazed that it was so. Perhaps Westerners have suffered from a lack of nurturing, while at the same time physical needs have been more than adequately met. Watching television with the family on the same sofa doesn't really count as being a loving exchange, and it does not equal a hug. I should make it clear that when I refer to loving oneself I am not talking about a spending spree at the shopping mall, which literally spoils us. Countless wealthy people will testify to the lack of long-term satisfaction that brings. Rather, I am talking about being aware of, and able to hear and act on, the messages from your heart. We all need to honor what makes our heart sing and to follow its spiritual guidance to allow this chakra to open.

Color

The color of Anahata chakra is green. The acupuncture point yutang ("jade hall") is in the center of the chest. I believe this point was named for the bright grass-green color that this chakra radiates. Tara, the Tibetan goddess of compassion, is green. Green has a calming effect— something you will know if you have ever felt exceptionally peaceful after a walk in the countryside. Tibetan monks write on green paper for its restful effect when their eyes feel strained. (I recommend people change the background color on their computer screens to green for this same reason.)

You may sometimes also experience a rose pink or gold color at Anahata when you do practices to open this chakra.

Element

Called the "gateway of the winds," Anahata relates directly to breathing, and to the lungs, so the associated element of this chakra is air. It is interesting that we can live without food for weeks, without water for days, but without air we die in just minutes. However, the essential element of Anahata is more than just air. Prana is the spark of life force within the air we breathe. The lungs,

in the metal element (see pranayama techniques, pages 137–43), rule our ability to connect with our earthly fathers and with the guiding wisdom of the heavens, our spirituality. Whenever we practice pranayama, breath control, we activate Anahata, even as we also activate other chakras with specific breaths.

Sense

Walking in the fields after a day's writing last week I stood for about ten minutes transfixed by the sight of a cow licking her calf. Her tenderness and devotion, the bliss on both their faces, seemed to me to sum up the energy of Anahata, characterized by the sense of touch. Scientists have proved that stroking a cat reduces blood pressure, while petting dogs brings much joy to people in hospitals and nursing homes.

We can refine our sense of touch easily. Pause now and touch the various surfaces around you, feeling the different textures of each. Then close your eyes and gently touch your face. Take plenty of time to explore the shapes, hills and crests of your features. The lightest, most fleeting of touches as we greet or part is transformative. A survey was done of people standing by a phone booth, asking strangers if they could spare change. When they were touched, however imperceptibly, people always found the time to check their change.

Age

The time when the energy Anahata is at its strongest is between the ages of 21 and 28. The traditional symbol of the rite of passage for a 21-year-old person is being given the key to the door: at this stage we are also potentially given the key to Anahata. With firm foundations in the lower three chakras already established, we should now be ready for the challenges of this phase: committed relationships, marriage, children and a vocation rather than just a job.

At some stage you have probably experienced the swelling in the heart chakra, almost a physical pain, of falling in love. Marriage or entering into an emotionally committed relationship requires that we elevate our love to embrace the needs of another, at the same time as

The symbol of Anahata

The 12 vermilion petals of the lotus, each inscribed with a Sanskrit symbol, surround two triangles superimposed on each other forming a hexagonal star. The upward-pointing triangle represents Shiva and the three higher chakras; the downward-pointing triangle, Shakti and the three lower chakras. They also indicate inhalation and exhalation. A symbol of perfect balance, it is traditionally colored smoky gray, like incense rising in a draft of air. In the center is a bana linga like a crescent moon, to represent the psychic blockage within. It is set in a golden triangle said to be as lustrous as 10 million flashes of lightning—indicating the explosion of divine light that can be seen when the vishnu granthi is untied and the heart chakra opens.

The deer or antelope at the bottom of the symbol refers to the lightness of physical substance in the air element—like the leap of the deer ridden by Avayu, vedic god of the winds.

Deities—Isa, Kakini

Isa is an aspect of Shiva, Lord of Speech. Depicted as shining white, or brick red, this deity has three eyes and two arms. He makes the gesture of dispelling fears with one hand while granting boons with the other. When we meditate on Isa we become like him, able to "protect and destroy the world" at the same time.

The goddess Kakini is shining yellow in color. She carries a noose reminding us not to get caught up in spiritual expectation—which, like trying to watch a pot boil, is sure to delay progress. The skull she holds tells us to maintain a pure mind. Her two other hands make the same gestures as Isa, dispelling fears (palm forward) and granting boons (palm up).

honoring the messages from our own heart. We need plenty of energy in the heart chakra to achieve that.

At no other time are we challenged quite so strongly to give out to others than when we become parents. Between the ages of 21 and 28 is the time acupuncturists recommend as being the healthiest to conceive a baby, as this is when the parents' chi is at its strongest. Those first few months of getting up night after night to feed and change your baby put a whole new spin on the concept of unconditional love. This is when partners are challenged to nurture each other, when so much is given out to the constantly demanding new person in their lives. The world often takes on a new dimension when we realize that we would willingly sacrifice ourselves, throw ourselves in front of a car, to save our child. And we certainly need the flexibility of the air element as we juggle the school run with shopping, working and running a household. So what helps us through it? The baby's smile, completely without artifice, little arms stretching out to be held. And most importantly, the compassion and love of balanced energy in Anahata.

When work is a vocation, not just a job, the heart chakra is content. It is not an uncommon occurrence for city professionals to ditch their high-flying lifestyles in order to enlist in teacher training courses or volunteer work in different countries around the world. These people have learned that it is spiritual contentment that counts, not a status car in the garage. People who are single, or who have no children, can benefit the heart chakra with dedicated work, especially if it is with children.

Physical connections

Anahata rules the heart, upper back, thorax, breasts, lungs, blood and circulation, skin, immune system, arms and hands.

The heart is the most important organ associated with this chakra, pumping blood around the body, delivering nutrients to every cell and cleansing your entire system. The lungs are part of this same system, delivering fresh oxygen to the blood and removing carbon dioxide in return. Babies are nurtured by the mother's breasts.

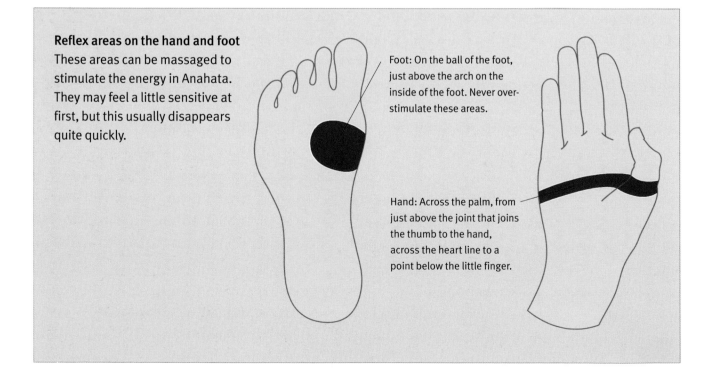

Reflex areas on the hand and foot
These areas can be massaged to stimulate the energy in Anahata. They may feel a little sensitive at first, but this usually disappears quite quickly.

Foot: On the ball of the foot, just above the arch on the inside of the foot. Never over-stimulate these areas.

Hand: Across the palm, from just above the joint that joins the thumb to the hand, across the heart line to a point below the little finger.

The abundant nerve cells in our skin enable us to feel and to touch. The Chinese view the skin as another lung, and we all know that our skin has to be able to breathe or we will die. There are many forms of chi/prana. The wei chi circulates over the surface of the skin during the day, regulating the opening and closing of the pores and preventing invasion by pathogens. At night, triggered by our eyes closing, the wei chi goes deep into the body to restore the vital organs, including the lungs and the heart. Our well-being is compromised, therefore, when we stay up into the small hours.

Immunity is also boosted by love given and received. I rarely treated just the symptoms of patients—which would bring only temporary relief. When a patient had "lost heart," treating points in the region of the heart chakra would not only cure their symptoms, it would also revive their spirits.

Good, unrestricted breathing is crucial to the sound functioning of Anahata and it can release long-held feelings, allowing the opening of this chakra (see Angel Wings, pages 110–11).

Gland

The governing gland in this chakra is the thymus. The thymus gland regulates growth, controls the lymph and strengthens the immune system and is directly affected by energy in Anahata.

Sound

Any music that lifts the heart when heard. It could be classical music, chanting, hymns, devotional music, and so on. All will activate Anahata. It is not unusual for music to move some people to tears.

Vowel

Ah, as in the word scarf, sung in the key of F, is the vowel sound of Anahata. This can be chanted gently, making a higher pitched *Ah* sound.

Mantra

The mantra of Anahata chakra is Yam (pronounced yang); when you chant this mantra the tongue rests within the mouth in midair. Focus on the center of the heart as you chant it. Done properly, it will vibrate the heart, opening up any blocks there and freeing energy to flow upward.

Gemstones

As before, be intuitive when it comes to choosing a gemstone, but rose quartz, watermelon tourmaline, kunzite, emerald, jade, green aventurine, malachite and chrysoprase are all associated with this chakra. Any of these stones can be placed on your chest between the breasts while you lie relaxing.

The stones can also be worn near the heart chakra most conveniently as a pendant, which is also very protective. Many people in China wear a small jade pendant for its benefits. (I sometimes tuck a small bright-green chrysoprase into my bra right above my heart.)

Aromatherapy oils

Attar of roses, bergamot, melissa, geranium and clary sage all activate this chakra. Choose an oil you like and dab a few drops on your chest. Why not make a mixture of a base oil, such as almond, and a few drops of Anahata oils, and massage a friend's hands with it?
Caution: Always check beforehand that the oils are suitable to use if you are breastfeeding or pregnant— clary sage should be avoided during pregnancy. Never use neat bergamot oil before exposure to the sun.

Foods

Natural foods, such as fruits, nuts, seeds and yogurt, which are gentle (sattvic) foods, calm us and support the energy in Anahata.

Balanced energy

This person radiates love and compassion, kindness, generosity and tolerance: I can give no better example than His Holiness the Dalai Lama. In his typically modest way, he calls himself a "simple Buddhist monk" and says all he does is practice loving kindness. People strong in the heart chakra have the ability to change the world around them; their lives are an expression of divine love. People with strong energy in Anahata have the natural ability to heal others; sometimes merely to be in their presence is healing. These are what Buddhists call "bodhisattvas," or enlightened people (see page 7).

Bodhisattvas are motivated by nothing other than pure compassion and love, and will endure any manner of suffering if, by doing so, they can help another person. The training of a bodhisattva begins by generating the "Six Perfections": generosity, ethics, patience, effort, concentration and wisdom. (I watched a care worker one day washing my mother's feet. The tenderness with which she cleaned and dried those old, calloused feet was extremely moving and I realized I was in the presence of a bodhisattva.)

Unbalanced or blocked energy

Physically there may be heart and circulation problems, lung disease such as asthma, bronchitis and other breathing problems if there is a blockage at this chakra. There may be a choice to smoke—a truly unloving act to oneself. Sometimes the chest looks armored, when the person habitually hardens their feelings or withholds them. Depression, or the inability to put one's heart into things, often collapses the chest, making the person look shrivelled and deflated.

Emotionally there can be a whole range of problems: hard-heartedness, lack of forgiveness, possessiveness, selfishness and cruelty. There may also be profoundly abusive behavior and the misuse of love. People suffering here may feel unworthy, dependent and needy. Sometimes melancholic, they may want to give love, but fear rejection. Another form of imbalance may mean giving is excessive, and with an expectation of return, or with an inability to receive. Too much emotion can tip over into oversympathy and anxiety, gushing behavior, wild mood swings. Think of the air element, and the expression "a fit of the vapors." This is often a lonely person, experiencing life as being full of sadness, their exchanges with other people full of "woundology," churning over the past.

Where this involves a perceived lack of mothering, it is as well to do a visualization of yourself as a tiny infant. Whatever you think of your mother, she probably got up night after night to feed you, care for and clean you. She cleaned your clothes and washed your dirty feet for years. The vishnu granthi is released by forgiveness.

Suggestions for balancing Anahata

- Practice loving kindness at all times.
- Learn to tune in to your heart's guidance and to trust it.
- Follow your first response, which is usually generous.
- Take time to enjoy nature, and practice walking gently on the Earth.
- Recycle whenever and whatever you can.
- Fill a vase with pink flowers.
- Notice when you become judgmental and lack compassion.
- Place a few drops of the appropriate aromatherapy oils on your chest.
- Read the poems of Rumi.
- Listen to uplifting music.
- Give a gift, and forget about it.
- Notice how much you receive from others.
- Thank the attendant when you use the facilities.
- End each day by writing down five things you feel grateful for.
- Chant *Ah* in the key of F, or the mantra Yam.
- Lie down and relax with one of the chakra's associated gemstones on your chest or between your breasts.
- Find it in your heart to forgive someone who you feel has wronged you.
- Live in the present.
- Do the postures for Anahata (see pages 110–14).
- Practice pranayama regularly (see pages 137–43).
- Try the visualization for Anahata (see page 154).

VISHUDDHA = TO PURIFY

Location
Throat

Purpose
Communication, creativity

Color
Pale turquoise/sky blue

Element
Ether

Symbol
16-petalled lotus

Age
28–35 years of age

Mantra
Ham

Vowel
Eh, as in the word raise

Balanced energy
Truthful
Clear spoken
Reflective
Inspiring/inspired
Creative
Imaginative
Non-judgmental
Honest about own
weaknesses
Independent
Aware of subtle dimensions
Good communicator
Contented

**Unbalanced or blocked
energy**
Poor communication
Overtalkative
Judgmental
Grating tone, stuttering and
so on
Dishonest
Lacking creativity
Uninspiring
Arrogant
Indecisive
Dependent
Unfeeling

Location

Vishuddha chakra is located in the throat. The chakra radiates from the dip between the inner collarbones, up to the Adam's apple in a man, from a level between the 3rd and 5th cervical vertebrae.

Purpose

This, the fifth main chakra, rules the aspects of communication and creativity. Here, creativity is on a more transpersonal level than at Svadisthana, the second chakra (see pages 32–9). Svadisthana, although also connected with creativity, expresses it on a more personal, physical level.

Whenever we speak, or communicate with such forms of creativity as painting, music or writing, we have the potential to set aside the ego and reach out from a more spacious, universally interconnected place. In this place we are able to hear our inner voice and receive guidance from the cosmos. You probably have experienced the complete absorption and calm that can overcome you when painting a scene, for example, or you suddenly hear the words to a song or a poem in your head. Transpersonal creativity comes through us, and we experience feelings that are like a vehicle for something larger than just ourselves.

The lesson to be learned at Vishuddha is to have faith and trust in divine guidance. When Vishuddha chakra opens fully, an unshakable trust in the inner voice develops, resulting in a deeper understanding of life. Information from subtler spheres and higher dimensions is always reliable (which is one way to check it out)—the trouble is we often find the messages inconvenient so our instinct is to ignore them. More often than not, this is because it requires us to make changes in our lives, sometimes radical ones. When, for example, did you last say "I knew I should not have done …"? When Vishuddha energy is strong, when we hear that inner voice, we can say "You choose, I'll follow, and trust that everything will be all right." In other words: thy will be done.

Thus, Vishuddha governs divine will, as distinct from personal will. At the base chakra, when we are infants, it seems as if everyone has authority over us. In the third chakra, we find our own authority. Acting from a place where personal will is guided by divine authority gets the best results … and how much easier life is when we give up the battleground of personal will.

Having faith allows us to remain true to ourselves and to others, whatever decisions we make. Vishuddha offers us the potential to foresee the consequences of all of our decisions, so that it becomes impossible to lie either to ourselves or to other people. Any incident of dishonesty or withholding of forgiveness can inhibit the ability for Vishuddha to open. When we forgive we retrieve energy from the past (where the betrayal or insult is endlessly rerunning)

and bring it forward into the present time to clear the decks to permit better communication to take place.

Vishuddha rules speech. Think of the many ways we communicate with our voice box: we laugh, cry, sing, chant, whisper, shout, scream, and wail. Hopefully we speak from the heart succinctly and honestly, without giving out a lot of hot air. Subtle meanings are conveyed with the slightest change in tone. (I have a friend who keeps her feelings well hidden, but I always know how she's feeling just by the tone of her voice.)

These tones are highly significant. Specifically, there are five that convey a whole range of information about a person: the laughing voice of fire, the weeping voice of metal, the groaning of water, the singing of earth and the shouting of wood. All the tones of the five elements take on an extreme form when they are out of balance. The shout of wood becomes louder, or a whisper, the kind of person you always have to strain to hear. The laugh of fire becomes excessive and inappropriate ("my mother just died, ha ha ha") or completely flat and joyless. The singing voice of earth goes to extremes or may become a monotone. The weeping sound of metal imbalance can be extremely quivery, just as if the person is actually crying, and the groan of a water imbalance grows deeper. Whenever I hear a shouting voice—the kind that is audible above all others in a crowded room—I know the person will likely have problems with anger, with their tendons and ligaments, be prone to gallbladder and liver disease, and may have trouble hearing.

Silence also nurtures Vishuddha chakra. It enables us to experience the spaciousness of Akasha, its element, allowing us to hear the inner voice with the ear of the higher mind. You will find that as Vishuddha develops you become more and more telepathic. You stretch out a hand to pick up the phone, it rings, and you find it is the person you were about to call. E-mails cross. You answer a question that has not yet been vocalized—mind meets mind directly. Some people find that they hear messages from people long dead. Dreams become inspirational and carry clear guidance. Life becomes full of synchronicity and coincidences. You may also become aware of your true mission in life.

Artists and musicians tend to have a concentration of energy in the fifth chakra. And when they connect with the purest level of creativity, their art is transcendent, sending a shiver down your spine. Conversely, a sure way for creativity to be stifled is to allow Vishuddha to become entangled with ego-related concerns, such as money, fame and fear. Western music developed from devotional Gregorian/Ambrosian chants; paintings were originally spiritual, conveying on a cave wall the spirit of animal and hunter. Some rock paintings in South Africa appear to portray an aura shining upward from elongated heads. Modern South Africans recognize what is happening in these ancient paintings and say it is exactly what happens when they go into a trance during ceremonial dances.

When Vishuddha chakra fully opens, the person is often a wonderful orator, with a beautiful and harmonious voice. You feel fully heard by such a person, and are moved by what is said to you. People with free-flowing energy here can also appear to communicate without words, their eyes drawing you in. His Holiness the Dali Lama draws huge crowds wherever he speaks, as did Jesus and Mohammed.

Vishuddha chakra functions in conjunction with two of the minor chakras: Lalana, which is located at the base of the nasal orifice, and Bindu Vishargha, found at the

The symbol of Vishuddha

The yantra here is a silver crescent, within a white, full-moon circle surrounded by 16 blue-gray lotus petals. The crescent is the symbol of the cosmic sound, nadam, and represents purity. Inside the circle is an akasamandala (yantra of a downward-pointing triangle) with a white circle within containing the Sanskrit symbol for Ham. The animal is the mighty elephant, like Muladhara, the first chakra, but this time the moon-white Airavata, vehicle of the god Indra, is unrestrained by a collar: servitude transformed into service.

Deities—Sadasiva and Sakti Sakini

Sadasiva is androgynous and is known as the "Ever Beneficent." Half the body is white, representing Shiva, and half gold, representing Sakti. He/she has five faces, each with three eyes, representing smell, taste, sight, touch, sound and the union of the five elements. He/she has ten arms, and wears a garland of snakes and a tiger skin. Sadasiva carries nine items and makes the fear-dispelling gesture known as abhaya mudra.

A noose (pasa) represents the danger of becoming caught up in spiritual pride.

A goad (ankusa) reminds us that we all need to make further effort.

The great snake, Nagendra, represents wisdom.

A trident (sula) represents the unity of the physical/etheric and causal bodies.

A flame (dahana), represents the fires of the great dormant transcendental energy Kundalini.

A bell (ghanta) represents the quality of inner hearing.

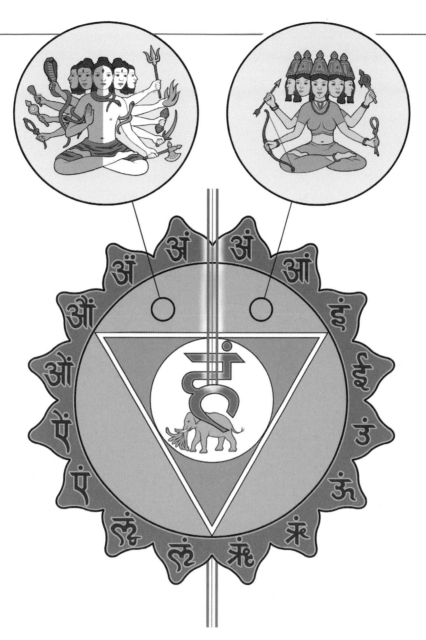

A diamond scepter (vajra) symbolizes the quality of indestructibility.

A sword (khadga) reminds us that we need to learn to discriminate.

A battle-ax (tanka) representing the cutting away of old aspects of the self.

The free hand faces forward, dispelling fear.

Sakti Sakini is an aspect of Gauri, mother of the universe, and she is sometimes clothed in yellow, representing light, sometimes sky blue with a green bodice, and with pale rose skin. The other half of Shiva's body, she carries a bow and arrow, a noose and a goad. She has the power to bestow psychic powers and speaks to us through our dreams.

top of the brain toward the back of the head. This is where Western monks shave and Eastern monks keep a topknot. It also connects with the rear throat chakra, which opens backward and has almost identical functions, as explained in the next chapter.

Color

Vishuddha chakra is the color of a clear blue sky, but it has also been described as being turquoise blue, silvery blue, like moonlight rippling on calm water, cyan blue and a silver greenish blue. To activate the energy of Vishuddha, wear a sky blue scarf around your throat, or a turquoise necklace. Then, on those occasions when you want to be heard, it will help you speak from your inner voice.

Element

The element associated with Vishuddha is Akasha/ether. Akasha is boundless space, infinite sky, carrying all other elements. It also carries subtle energy/sound vibrations. Sometimes it is described as astral light. Focus your energy in Vishuddha by lying on the grass and gazing up at the infinite space of a clear blue sky.

Akasha is also inner spaciousness, which allows us to reflect on our thoughts and actions, helping us to discriminate between the functions of the emotional, ethereal and the physical bodies. Hence, thoughts are no longer dominated by feelings and physical sensations, freeing us to be more objective, and to receive messages in the higher mental body (see pages 12–13).

Sense

The sense associated with Vishuddha is hearing. Have you ever noticed that there is no complete silence? Try it now, by closing your eyes and listening. Wait for sounds to arrive. Do you notice that between sounds—birds, car doors slamming, distant voices and so on—there is a constant background hum? This is what the yogis call "nadam," and it is said to be the sound of your own cells vibrating. When Vishuddha opens this becomes clearer, like a ringing bell, and this is often mistaken for tinnitus. The yogis use this sound as a tool for meditation (see

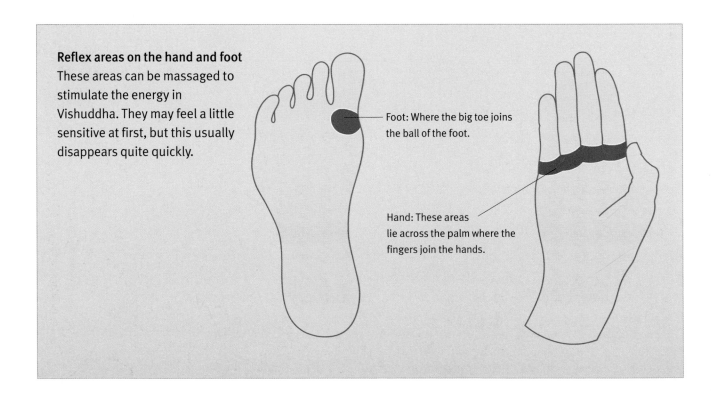

Reflex areas on the hand and foot
These areas can be massaged to stimulate the energy in Vishuddha. They may feel a little sensitive at first, but this usually disappears quite quickly.

Foot: Where the big toe joins the ball of the foot.

Hand: These areas lie across the palm where the fingers join the hands.

page 150), strongly activating Vishuddha. Chanting mantras and the bija sounds also have a powerful effect on this chakra.

Age

The time when this chakra's energy is at its strongest is between the ages of 28 and 35. Jobs, marriages, where and how we live, friendships, all come under scrutiny as we reflect on whether they will serve us well for the latter part of our lives. Vishuddha energy may manifest at first as a kind of restlessness—of not knowing what we want to be when we grow up. We do our job, but is it our vocation? We may feel the urgent need to nurture our inner spirit in some way. Couples may suddenly find they want to communicate on a deeper level, which can throw the relationship into crisis if it is not honored— bear in mind that the sense of this chakra is hearing. We need to learn to be heard and to hear equally.

Physical connections

Vishuddha rules the throat, neck, nape of neck, vocal cords, voice, bronchial tubes, trachea, esophagus, jaw, arms, nose, teeth, thyroid glands and hearing.

Whenever you get a sore throat, ask yourself: "What am I avoiding saying to someone?" The throat is fine-tuned to pick up these things, and will give us a nudge with soreness, tonsillitis or hoarseness—we may even lose our voice completely. Sometimes the question might be: "Who is the pain in my neck?" (I've lost count of the times I would make this suggestion to patients, to see a knowing smile spread across their faces.)

I spoke earlier about the harmonious voice of someone with an open Vishuddha chakra—when there are problems, the voice can take on a strangulated or a quavering tone. Try stretching out your neck forward and read this sentence aloud, and as you finish the sentence lengthen the back of your neck, tucking your chin in slightly. Can you hear how your voice softens?

Have you ever noticed how people will go completely deaf on you when they are highly stressed or in a panic? Whatever you say to assuage their fears falls on deaf ears. The kidney meridian rules hearing and fear. Again, fear

is destructive to the healthy functioning of this chakra and will block its opening and the free flow of energy.

Glands

The thyroid and parathyroid are the glands associated with this chakra. Thyroid problems, over- or under-active, are associated with the fifth chakra, as are parathyroid problems, such as cysts and tumors.

Sound

All forms of spiritual chanting, such as Taissé and Gregorian, stimulate the throat chakra, as does singing hymns, or just singing generally. This is most effective if done early in the morning, between 3 and 5 a.m., as this is when the lung meridian peaks in energy. This is probably why there is a tradition in religious communities to begin devotions early in the morning.

Vowel

Eh, as in the word raise, sung in the key of G, is the vowel sound of Vishuddha. This can be chanted as a mantra or repeated silently, and it is especially effective used while doing the fish posture, or asana (see pages 117).

Mantra

The mantra for the fifth chakra is Ham. Form an oval with your lips and, expelling air outward from the throat, sound the mantra, pronouncing it "hang." This vibrates the brain and speeds the flow of cerebral spinal fluid to the throat, making the voice more melodious.

Gemstones

Aquamarine, turquoise, chalcedony, celestite, sodalite and pale sapphire are the gemstones associated with this chakra. Located in an area where it can easily be stimulated, wear your chosen gemstone on a chain— silver is a good choice —so that the stone sits in the hollow of your neck.

Aromatherapy oils

Sage, eucalyptus, lavender, sandalwood, neroli, myrrh and chamomile all activate Vishuddha. Dab a drop of the oil you are drawn to in the hollow of your neck, or first mix it in a base oil, such as almond. There is an acupuncture point here, known as "pearl jade"—a good description of the color of Vishuddha.

Foods

Light sattvic foods support the energy of Vishuddha, and I would recommend the lightest of foods—ones that encourage a contemplative, right-brain, calm state. These are the so-called sattvic foods of ayurveda: grapes, salads, herbs and so on. A little plain yogurt with a teaspoon of honey for the throat is perfect.

Balanced energy

People with balanced energy in this chakra are truly inspiring to be with and are naturally looked up to by others. They always tell the truth and they speak clearly. In fact, they can communicate well with all types of people even without speaking. Their ability to be reflective means that they are completely non-judgmental. Their lives are creative and inspiring to others, and they bring imaginative solutions to disputes.

Highly psychic, they may have many esoteric abilities, such as telepathy, clairaudience, clairvoyance, and yet will make light of them as long as the other chakras are well balanced. They impress with an ability to own their failings and with the directness of their honesty. They cannot be manipulated by others and they are clear about decisions that are made under the influence of an acknowledged higher power. They find it comparatively easy to meditate and may develop many powers in this, such as depriving themselves of food or drink or developing extraordinary control over their bodies. Finally, their contentment is an example to us all.

Unbalanced or blocked energy

This might be the person with verbal diarrhea, the one who never lets anyone else have any airtime, while gossiping or shouting down other people's opinions. They may be dogmatic, judgmental and arrogant. They may also hold inconsistent or unreliable views.

There will be poor communication between mind and body leading to problems either connected with their feelings and how they have an impact on the body, or a shutting off from their feelings altogether. The person may be very hard on themselves, or go along with other people's opinions of them. This may detach them from their true selves, sometimes masked with a multitude of words. Language may be coarse, argumentative, blatant or cool and businesslike, without emotion.

Weak/blocked energy here can manifest itself as a stutter or in dishonesty. Physically, there will be issues around the throat area, as previously described, and a general rigidity around the neck and shoulders. They may be tensed up around the ears in an unconscious gesture of protection.

The spiritual energy may become bogged down in the head, or in the lower chakras. It has been known for spiritual leaders to develop an imbalance when too much time is spent developing the higher centers at the cost of the lower. We need to use our discrimination, and to be wary if they start buying fleets of limousines.

Suggestions for balancing Vishuddha

- Spend time in silence, and listen regularly for the inner voice.
- Set aside time for reflection about your life and direction. Ask yourself if you are happy with its course.
- Lie on the grass on a warm day and gaze up at a clear blue sky and contemplate the ether.
- Sit by a lake, pond or by the sea in the moonlight and watch the light reflected in the water.
- Wear the color turquoise around your throat as a necklace, scarf or collar.
- Eat pure, sattvic foods.
- Practice being completely honest with yourself and with others.
- After a social event, reflect on what you said, and how you expressed it.
- Listen to the tone of your voice and make adjustments if necessary.
- From time to time throughout the day, lengthen the back of your neck, by tucking your chin into your chest slightly.
- Chant *Eh* in the key of G, or the mantra Ham. Join a choir or sing in the shower.
- Try the visualization for Vishuddha (see page 154).
- Do the postures (asanas) for Vishuddha (see pages 115–17).
- Practice pranayama regularly (see pages 137–43).
- Take up a hobby where your deep inner creativity may flourish.
- Speak up for yourself.
- Think of a person or people you need to forgive and either address them personally, or write them a letter of forgiveness and burn it.
- Look at how you might increase creativity in your work.
- Next time you have a sore throat, ask: "What am I avoiding saying to someone?"

ajna gateway of liberation

AJNA = TO PERCEIVE, TO KNOW

Location
Brow

Purpose
Intuition, self-mastery

Color
Indigo

Symbol
A two-petalled lotus

Mantra
Om

Vowel
E, as in easy

Balanced energy
Clarity
Contentment
Discernment
Detachment
Psychic
Intuitive
Natural healers
Wise
Insightful
Respected
Strong faith

Unbalanced or blocked energy
Rationalist
Doubtful
Mistrustful
Lacking insight
Lacking discrimination
Intellectually arrogant
Materialistic
Isolated
Lacking discernment
Attached
Unspiritual

Location

This chakra, Ajna, known commonly as the third eye chakra, is located slightly above and between the eyebrows and projects forward from the pituitary gland, but it is also linked with the pineal. It is paired with the minor Soma chakra, which sits just above it (see page 88).

Purpose

Dwelling place of the subtle mind, when Ajna opens fully it is equivalent to receiving the advantage a sighted person would have in the midst of a crowd of the blind. This is a person of knowledge and self-mastery. Most of us live our lives and make decisions guided by minds tainted with unresolved emotional patterns, hurts, anger, prejudices and the opinions of others, which add up to give us a view of the world that is as distorted as that seen in a funhouse mirror. This is the state of duality.

People with strong energy in this the sixth chakra view the world with absolute clarity, understanding instinctively the inter-connection between all things. They have detachment, sometimes misunderstood as lack of compassion, possessing an ability not to get caught up in distorting emotions. When Ajna opens it is as if we slip off a chain mail of delusions that trapped us in limited thinking. When the last of the three psychic knots, the rudra granthi at Ajna, unravels (see page 20), we are truly

liberated. Many psychic abilities develop and there is a knowing that surpasses anything previously experienced.

People with an active Ajna chakra are always guided by their intuition. As speech is to the throat center, so vision is to the brow—this is the realm of the seer, the wise one, possessing wisdom beyond the norm.

Clairvoyance is strong, visualization second nature. The consequences of any action are known in advance, and understood—knowledge of the past and future as clear as of the present. Powers may include clairaudience (hearing guidance from the cosmos) or clairsentience (receiving information through touch). Telepathy will be very strong, life full of synchronicity.

Let me tell you a story. Once there was a young monk who thought he would test the extraordinary powers of his teacher, Lama Yeshe of Kopan monastery. It was a hot day and the meditation room was crowded. The young monk visualized handing Lama Yeshe a tall glass of freshly squeezed orange juice. Lama Yeshe paused in his lecture, looked straight at him and said "thank you my son, thank you so much …" and then continued.

We cannot open the door to this powerful chakra by effort alone. To experience its eternal, supreme blissful state, free from the fear of death, with profound inner knowing, we have first to develop a deep enough understanding of the forces concealed behind it. When we are strong enough to

embrace this much light, it happens spontaneously, and can happen at any age. The knot unravels and we experience the ecstasy of non-duality. All knowledge exists—but, like energy stored in the seed of a plant, it is hidden from the understanding of most people. For the enlightened, everything suddenly becomes clear, cause and effect known—much as some people describe near-death experiences.

Color

The color associated with Ajna is indigo. However, it will radiate yellow in a person experiencing rational, intellectual thoughts, and violet when extrasensory perception is active.

Ajna is activated whenever indigo is worn anywhere on the body. You can also surround yourself with flowers, such as purple iris, and burn deep-blue candles.

Element

None associated. While no element is associated, you could say that light rays are the element of Ajna.

Sense

People with an open Ajna chakra usually experience a heightening of all their senses. Extrasensory perception (ESP) is very strong and they have strong radar for other people's feelings.

Age

None applicable. The spontaneous awakening of Ajna can occur at any age, and there are many stories of enlightened children—the Dalai Lama for one. Its opening occurs through grace, not effort, although the way we live our lives makes this more or less likely.

Physical connections

Ajna rules the eyes, base of skull, face, nose, sinuses, cerebellum and the central nervous system. Since the brain and nervous system are under the control of Ajna, we should look at the dual hemispheres. The right brain, associated with the left, female side of the body, is active when we are in a creative, lateral-thinking mode, quiet and focused, and is particularly active when meditating. The left brain, associated with the right, male side of the body, becomes more active when we are in a logical, active frame of mind. The ancient yogis used to balance both sides of the brain using alternate nostril breath (see page 143) and would breathe through the appropriate nostril for the task.

The brain commands movement of the physical body; the mind commands the energy body. Energy follows wherever we direct our thoughts, which is why we become so exhausted constantly reworking insults and injuries from the past, or projecting worries into the future. Focusing attention on Ajna helps us to live in the present moment, and gives our tired brains a rest.

The eyes and the nose are often affected if there is an energy imbalance in Ajna. There may be headaches, nightmares, delusional behavior and problems with the central nervous system.

Glands

Although a connection with the pineal gland has been demonstrated, given its role as the command center of the endocrine system, the ability to rejuvenate the entire body and the fact that it has two lobes—anterior and posterior—I favor the connection with the pituitary gland. Both glands are likely to be influenced by or to exert influence on Ajna.

Sound

It could be any music that expands and opens the mind, more usually classical music, puts us in the appropriate mental state for Ajna to open. The important thing is really to listen to and engage with the music, and let it lead you where it will. Our cells explode with color and light when the right note is played to them. If you experience music as irritating or "grating on you," then it probably is. The best advice is to switch it off or move to another room. You will recognize uplifting music as soon as you hear it.

Vowel

E, as in the word easy, sung in the key of A. Chant this as a mantra before you meditate.

Mantra

The mantra for this chakra is perhaps the best known of all, Om, sometimes called the pranava, and has the power to activate Ajna and raise Kundalini. It also stimulates the cerebellum and opens the central nervous system to cosmic vibrations, and should be treated with much respect. Om, or Aum, reflects the inner sound, nadam, the vibrating molecules of the universe or cosmic music. Focus for a moment or two on nadam. Then begin chanting by making a short, guttural "a" sound from the lowest area of the vocal tract. Allow the sound to develop into an "o" sound as you gradually move it to the higher regions of the vocal tract. Let it develop into a "u" sound as it resonates from the frontal regions of the vocal tract. Then as you close your mouth and intone the more nasal "m," the Aum is complete. Finish your chants by focusing again on the inner sound.

The symbol of Ajna

Although it is traditional to depict only two petals for this lotus, they overlay an invisible 48 others on either side. The two indicate that this is where male/female Ida and Pingala energies meet and terminate—only the central Sushumna, the most important of all the nadis/meridians (see pages 16–17), continues up to the crown of the head. They represent wings of transcendence, or the two snake heads of Ida and Pingala, the conjoining of the male and female energies. They also represent the primal duality that arises from our original unified state, and which is present in all things: the two hemispheres of the brain; our right and left eye; the two globes of the pituitary gland; our bilateral outer bodies. It is a reminder that even though the aura is ovoid and radiates outward, inside are subfields that flow in opposite directions up and down the subtle body.

The petals are traditionally white with the mantra Hang representing Shiva on one side, and Ksham, representing Shakti on the other, together meaning "I am that I am." Between the petals is a white circle, representing Shunya, the void, or pure existence, source of being and point of return. Inside the circle is a yantra of a golden, downward-pointing triangle with the mantra OM inside. Behind the mantra is the linga itara, which is white with streaks of lightning hinting at the extraordinary powers of Ajna. There is no animal associated with Ajna.

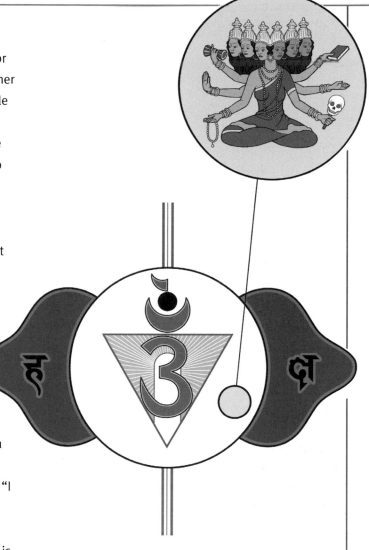

Deity—Sakti Hakini

Sakti Hakini combines a dual female/male aspect. She/he is moon-white with six red faces. The hands carry a drum (the pulse of life), a skull (reminding us to keep the mind empty), a mala (used to keep count when chanting mantras) and a book (representing wisdom), while the other two hands make the gestures for dispelling fear and granting boons.

Gemstones

Amethyst, purple apatite, azurite, calcite, sapphire, fluorite, lapis lazuli and opal are associated with Ajna. Gazing at any of these will activate the chakra, but try lying down with one of them on your forehead.

Aromatherapy oils

Try hyacinth, violet, rose geranium, jasmine, vetiver, basil, patchouli, rosemary or mint. Use the oils as previously described and dab a little on Ajna.

Foods

Black currants and blueberries are known to have beneficial effects on the eyes. And while fasting is also appropriate for activating Ajna, it should be done only under the direction of a properly qualified teacher. Never fast to lose weight.

Balanced energy

We find ourselves naturally drawn to people whose energy is balanced here. They command our respect without demanding it, and are often very humble. People will automatically seek their wise guidance, and trust their authority. I have often found them to be very light and humorous too, taking an exceptional delight in the world, living as they do in a state of blissful gratitude. Just to be in their presence is uplifting. People have been known to be healed simply by being near them and many of them have the power to do remote healing. Their auras are sometimes visible, even to people not used to seeing them, because they are so radiant, appearing like a halo around their heads. They also sometimes smell fragrant, like exquisite incense (the original meaning of the odor of sanctity).

When Ajna is open and balanced there is wisdom as opposed to knowledge, a sense of harmony in the world, calm and deep spirituality. Introspection is well integrated. Most people receive inspiration only in flashes from this center, the occasional transient experience, eureka moments when the mystical truth of a situation is known. A person with a fully open Ajna chakra lives in a state of constant heightened awareness

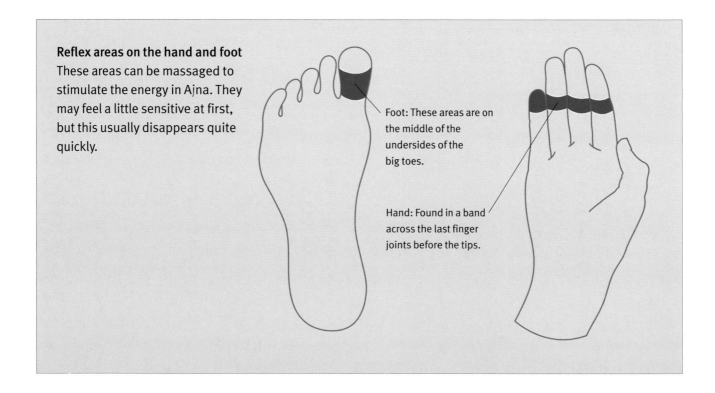

Reflex areas on the hand and foot
These areas can be massaged to stimulate the energy in Ajna. They may feel a little sensitive at first, but this usually disappears quite quickly.

Foot: These areas are on the middle of the undersides of the big toes.

Hand: Found in a band across the last finger joints before the tips.

and inspiration. As long as they maintain a balance with the lower, grounding chakras, they never abuse their abundant psychic powers.

Unbalanced or blocked energy

This person experiences life all on the material plane, seeking solace from possessions, unmotivated to look beyond the mundane. Their minds run on rational lines and deeper meanings are rejected. Top-heavy in intellectual pursuits, they may become arrogant about what they know. Setting aside little time for reflection, they believe in the world as they see it, and reject spirituality. This often leads to feelings of dissatisfaction, isolation and emptiness.

Mentally they may be depressed, have headaches and suffer from confusion and muddled thinking. They may have learning difficulties, poor vision, glaucoma or other eye problems, and sometimes neurological disturbances.

Suggestions for balancing Ajna

- Take time alone sitting quietly, reflecting.
- Gaze at a starry night sky and contemplate the void.
- Maintain a regular practice of yoga and meditation, or tai chi.
- Eat light, sattvic foods; always finish your meal feeling you could eat a little more.
- Avoid *oversleeping*. Follow the natural rhythms of the day.
- Practice generosity, and always think of others first.
- Become more conscious of your intuitions, and start recording them in a special notebook.
- Notice when coincidences happen, and record them.
- Look for the deeper meanings when surprises happen.
- Chant vowel sound *E* in the key of A, or the mantra Om (Aum).
- Touch a drop of the associated aromatherapy oils on your forehead when you meditate.
- Welcome silence in your life, stillness and solitude.
- Wear indigo blue, or gaze at one of the associated gemstones, or place one on your forehead while you lie relaxing.
- Smell your hands after running them through a mint bush.
- Get used to asking regularly for guidance from your higher self/cosmos.
- Practice the visualization for Ajna (see page 155).
- Do the yoga postures/exercises for Ajna (see pages 118–19).
- Remember to give thanks for your intuitions and to acknowledge that you had help.

sahasrara gateway of the void

SAHASRARA = THOUSAND-PETALLED

Location
Crown of the head

Purpose
Unity, bliss

Color
Violet

Symbol
A thousand-petalled lotus

Vowel
M, toned in the key of B

Open energy
Control of emotions
Clear concentration
Discernment
Effective action
Fulfilling goals
Unity of spiritual and
mundane world
Freedom of mind
Insightful
Healthy
Radiant
Modest
Humorous
Compassionate
Nonattachment

Dormant energy
Alienation
Depression
Obsessive thoughts
Egocentric
Fearful
Prideful
Attachments
Dissatisfaction
Illnesses
Exhaustion
Lacking connection with
the spirit
Swept away by emotions
Lacking motivation
Controlling
Ungenerous

Location

Traditionally said to be located on the crown of the head, Sahasrara can also be sensed. To do this, try holding your hand over your head, four finger-widths above the crown, for a few moments. The energy in Sahasrara "chakra" radiates upward, and it also receives universal energy down from the cosmos. Strictly speaking, Sahasrara is not really a chakra; rather, it is an area of divine consciousness waiting to be released.

Purpose

The purpose of Sahasrara is engendering unity and bliss. At Sahasrara we reach the summit of human spiritual potential. Its function is nothing less than union with the Divine, a merging of the self with the cosmic energies of the multiverse, bringing about an inner state of bliss or enlightenment.

Little is written about this chakra, this divine consciousness, because only the truly enlightened may know it and, paradoxically, they rarely speak of it.

At Ajna (see pages 64–9), Shakti and Shiva (Ida and Pingala, yin and yang) are united in the Sushumna (see pages 16–17). Here, where the Sushumna rises beyond the first six chakras following the line of the spine and arrives at the crown, united energy connects with cosmic/heavenly energy, offering the potential for ultimate knowing and liberation from the constraints of the mundane world.

Known as the "gateway of the void," the abode of Shiva, when Sahasrara opens there is a dissolution of the concepts of "you" and "I" giving an unparalleled understanding of the true nature of things. Sahasrara is said to shine with the brilliance of tens of millions of suns, with the coolness of tens of millions of moons. Descriptions that are meant to stretch the bounds of your imagination, for awareness is expanded here beyond description—it is vast, limitless knowledge outside of the realm of words or intellect. The Hindus call this state of enlightenment Moksha (liberation); the Buddhists, nirvana (the cessation of desire); Sufis, Boga (union with God); and the yogis, samadhi/union.

This union is the ultimate goal of all yogic practices. Yoga means "union"—it's not just a method of bending the body into peculiar shapes. Our aim should be toward this state of bliss through a path of gradual unfolding (see pages 12–13 and 21).

Color

Although the predominant color radiating from Sahasrara is violet, it synchronizes with all the colors and often radiates white and gold. It is often depicted in traditional religious paintings, particularly in icons, as a stylized golden halo surrounding the head of saints or of a holy person. It is sometimes visible to people who are not usually clairvoyant, glowing around the heads of deeply spiritual individuals.

Element

There is no specific element associated with Sahasrara.

Sense

There is no specific sense associated with Sahasrara.

Age

No age is attributable to Sahasrara, since enlightenment can occur at any age and arises by grace. There is the potential for any one of us to achieve it in our current lifetime. We have already experienced this state in small measure, as infants, before the fontanel closed. Have you ever noticed there is something very special about the aura of a new baby?

When a person dies, it is common for their pulses to become perfectly balanced, if only for the last few minutes. In Japan, this phenomenon is known as the last rays of the setting sun and I believe it may relate to a return to this state of bliss.

Physical connections

The cerebral cortex, brain and the whole body are associated with Sahasrara chakra. Therefore, you might reasonably suspect that a lack of harmony in Sahasrara is experienced whenever neurological disturbances are present.

Gland

The mysterious pineal gland (epiphysis) gets its name because of its pinecone shape, and it is the associated gland for Sahasrara. The pineal gland is also commonly known as the third eye. It is responsible for secreting melatonin into the bloodstream. It is this simple, though vitally important hormone that communicates light levels to various parts of the body. Melatonin controls our biological rhythms, affecting sleep and reproduction. Levels of melatonin in the blood rise sharply during the hours of darkness.

Only small in size, measuring approximately ⅓ inch (1 cm) in length in humans, the pineal gland is located on the midline, and is attached to the posterior end of the third ventricle in the brain. By the time puberty is under way, the pineal gland is already showing distinct signs of calcification. It seems to have a connection to our imagination and creativity, features that are so strong in small children. Is there perhaps a connection between the pineal calcifying and views and attitudes polarizing?

Sound

The sound of Sahasrara is silence.

Vowel

The vowel sound associated with Sahasrara is *M*, which should be toned in the key of B. (In India, M is considered to be a vowel.)

Mantra

Sahasrara has no mantra.

Gemstones

Clear quartz, amethyst, diamond, white jade, white tourmaline, snowy quartz, herkimer diamond, alexandrite and sapphire are all associated with Sahasrara. Any of them, whichever one chooses you, may be placed just above your crown while you lie on a mat in deep relaxation, or you can gaze at your chosen gemstone in meditation.

Aromatherapy oils

Place two or three drops of any of the following aromatherapy oils on the crown before meditation, or use the oils in a burner while you meditate: lavender, frankincense, rosewood or lotus. The resin of the olibanum tree is the classic incense to use.

Foods

There are no particular foods associated with Sahasrara chakra. People with an open Sahasrara eat moderately, and with compassion for other living things, taking in only what they need to survive.

Energy in Sahasrara

For this chakra, it is more appropriate to talk of the energy being either open or dormant.

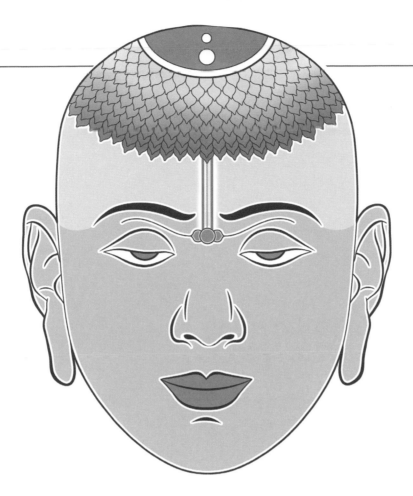

The symbol of Sahasrara

The shower of cosmic forces raining down on the individual is symbolized by a fully opened, multi-layered, thousand-petalled white lotus on the crown of the head, each layer containing 50 Sanskrit letters. The inner petals glow with white light interspersed with gold. In the pericarp of the lotus is a mandala of Surya and Chandra, the Sun and Moon.

Within the Moon mandala is a lightning-like triangle, said to be as fine as a one-hundredth part of a fiber of the lotus: inside that is the Nirvana-kala, as subtle as a one-thousandth part of the tip of a hair. The Nirvana-kala grants the power of divine knowledge and is as lustrous as the light from all the suns. Like the layers of an onion, inside the Nirvana-kala is the para bindhu (itself containing all that has been created) with Shakti and Shiva, and within that is the void. It is no accident that the symbol, too, is beyond simple depiction and is usually shown simply as an open lotus.

Deity — Shiva

Known as the "abode of Shiva," the masculine force, Sahasrara chakra is where the magnetic polarities of Shakti, the feminine force, mother of form, unites with Shiva, consciousness.

Open energy

When Sahasrara opens we are released from the prison of illusions that most of us inhabit; the spiritual and mundane world unite like nuclear fusion, transforming human consciousness.

This can happen quite suddenly, just as a piece of ripe fruit falls from the tree when its time has come. A regular spiritual discipline conducted over many years, and a life that is lived in consideration for other living things and for the planet, increase the possibility for attaining a state of enlightenment. We all enter this world at different stages of development—thus a baby may have many lifetimes of spiritual development behind it at birth and may be born enlightened or achieve this state at a very young age.

It sometimes happens that as Sahasrara gradually opens, people go through a spiritual crisis—a type of dark night of the soul—as the ego dissolves. When an onion grows, the outer layers rot and smell as they feed the growing shoot; in the same way, the lotus blossom develops and grows out of putrefying mud at the bottom of the pond. These crises when things look so muddy and rotten, making us feel confused, senseless, fearing annihilation or sometimes desiring it, are often messages to look inside more deeply. If the signs to rest and go deeper are ignored or mistaken, an opportunity may be missed.

The enlightened person is no longer affected by waves of conflicting emotions, giving them an aura of calm. Though sensitive to their own and other people's mental states, they are in control and experience deeper and more meaningful connections with others. Physically, the body is healthy, radiant. Similar to people with an open Ajna chakra, they have great powers of discernment and an air of reliable authority. Modest, humorous, compassionate, they are the spiritual leaders who do not seek the limelight or the trappings of fame. They probably follow a regular discipline, such as yoga, meditation or prayer, and are infinitely kind, generous and wise. Psychic abilities are strong: when they wish to know something they have only to direct their attention to it for answers to come.

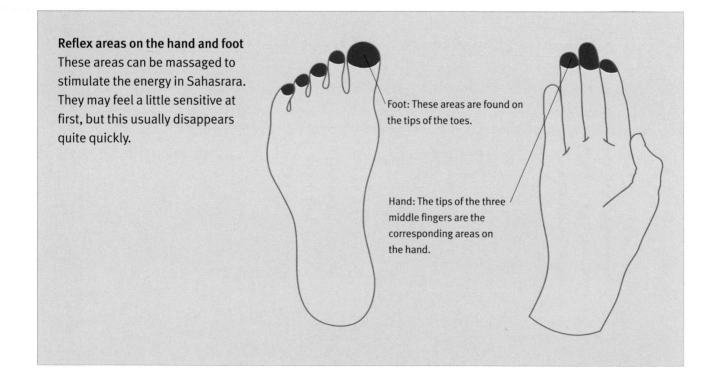

Reflex areas on the hand and foot
These areas can be massaged to stimulate the energy in Sahasrara. They may feel a little sensitive at first, but this usually disappears quite quickly.

Foot: These areas are found on the tips of the toes.

Hand: The tips of the three middle fingers are the corresponding areas on the hand.

When the crown chakra, Sahasrara, opens, any blocks in the lower six chakras dissolve and energy vibrates in all of them at the highest possible frequency. Cosmic energy being absorbed into the crown ceases and energy radiates upward and outward. At last, the true self is known—as if the individual has awoken from a dream. The heart opens and all is one, the Divine Being is within as without, the self part of the omnipresent pure Being.

There is a story of a student of Tibetan Buddhism asking an enlightened master, a Geshe lama, how he experienced the world. After all, the lama was always laughing. The lama clicked his fingers, and at once the gray scenery around them transformed into a heaven-like world of sunshine, flowers, fearless animals and birds and sparkling streams.

Dormant energy

For most of us, to varying degrees at least, anxieties, fears and doubts dominate at least some stages of our lives. These concerns could be about social status, health, abandonment, our finances, emotional life or whatever. There are health issues, depression, dissatisfaction, ambition—it's a struggle to imagine cosmic unity. We may lack the discipline to perform a regular spiritual practice, and ignore our intuitions from fear or lack of trust. We are unsettled by events around us, our lives seem to be full of frustration and tensions. What we should bear in mind is that the potential always exists for these things to be overcome. Enlightenment and, therefore, freedom from all of the above are possible for all of us.

Suggestions for opening Sahasrara

- Take time to experience nature, especially from the top of a mountain.
- Spend time in total silence.
- Go on regular retreats.
- Eat moderately, taking in only what you need.
- Sleep moderately.
- Practice living an ethical lifestyle.
- Keep up a regular practice of yoga, tai chi or similar.
- Practice pranayama regularly (see pages 137–43).
- Meditate regularly—at least once a day.
- Practice the visualization for Sahasrara (see page 155).
- Try the postures (asanas) on pages 120–3.
- Practice loving kindness at all times.

3 | the minor chakras

Today, knowledge of the seven major chakras is not uncommon; it is less usual, however, for people to know about the many minor chakras, and yet their healthy functioning is central to spiritual growth and healing. Janet Swan, a healer at the Cancer Help Center in Bristol, England, says that she doesn't even begin to work on the major seven until the energy in the minor chakras is released and flowing well, and that their free flowing seems to be a requirement for the seven majors to respond.

Each acupuncture point (and there are 327 on the 14 main meridians alone, as well as many head and ear points and others not on specific meridians) is a mini-chakra, some more powerful than others. It is not necessary to describe them all, but below I give details of some of the most significant minor chakras. Starting the journey at the south of the body map, below the feet, we will travel around them, up the body until we reach a point above the crown of the head.

Head chakras

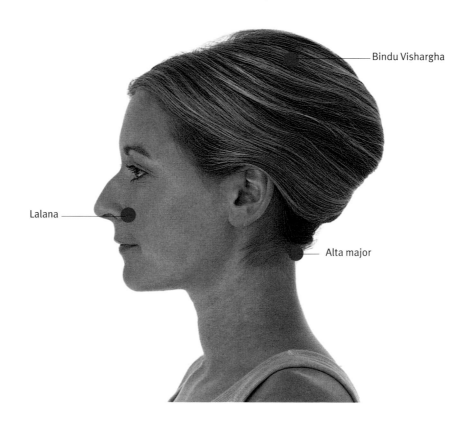

Bindu Vishargha

Lalana

Alta major

Whole-body chakras

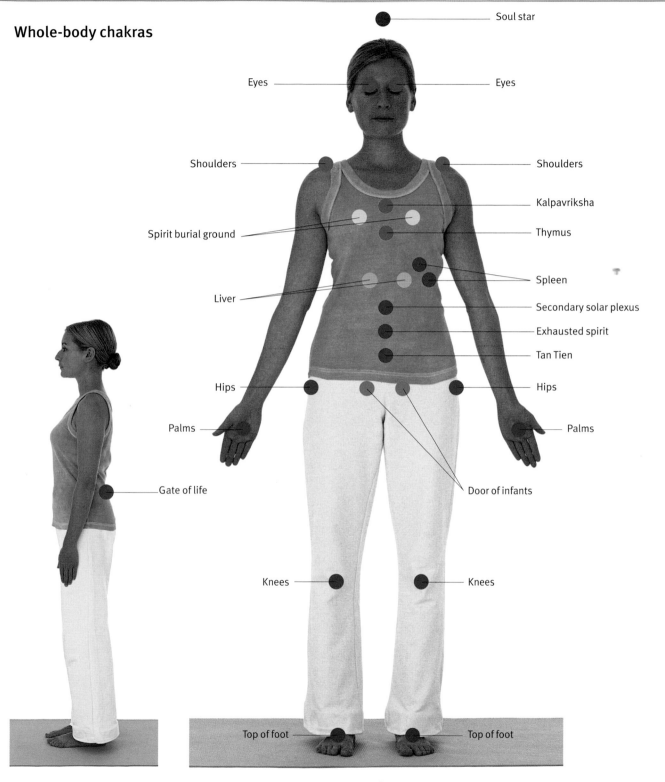

Soul star

Eyes — Eyes

Shoulders — Shoulders

Kalpavriksha

Spirit burial ground — Thymus

Liver — Spleen

Secondary solar plexus

Exhausted spirit

Tan Tien

Hips — Hips

Palms — Palms

Gate of life

Door of infants

Knees — Knees

Top of foot — Top of foot

Earth star

the exercises

It is extremely beneficial to activate the minor chakras using a variety of exercises—some physical and others that employ visualization techniques to take attention to specific locations. The exercises below and those on the following pages stimulate several important minor chakras. You can also use the warm-up exercises at the beginning of the next chapter.

EARTH STAR CHAKRA

About 9 inches (23 cm) below the feet, in a direct line with the base chakra and Sahasrara, Earth star gives us our grounding, connecting us to the earth's magnetic grid and focusing our energy. The higher spiritual energies require constant anchoring by this chakra. We could say: as below, so above.

1 Stand with your feet a comfortable hip-distance apart, close your eyes and visualize Earth star just below you, connecting you to the planet.

TOP OF FOOT CHAKRAS

Healers sense the energy of this chakra on the top of the foot, on the arch, either by holding the feet or placing their hands just above. Here lies the source point of the stomach meridian, Chungyan (Rushing Yang). The earth element meridians ground us, and we often feel anxious when they are blocked or weak. Directly below the arch, on the sole of the foot, is Yungchuan (bubbling spring), the first point on the kidney meridian, where an abundant flow of energy bubbles up to refresh us. I believe that healers connect through the foot to this point at the same time. Remembering that the water element helps us to express fear appropriately, balancing the energy flow in this chakra can make us feel less disconnected and fearful.

To summarize, blocked energy here may prevent people from achieving their full potential. They may feel insecure, as if the universe does not support them. The foot chakras are severely affected by radical health treatments, such as chemotherapy and radiotherapy, and they are often an area of weakness for the astrological air signs (Gemini, Aquarius and Libra). Pisceans also benefit from grounding.

1 Stand with your feet a comfortable hip-distance apart, spread your toes, balance your weight evenly on ball of the foot and heels and feel your connection to the ground.

2 Now close your eyes and imagine receiving an abundant flow of energy from the earth through Yungchuan on the soles of your feet.

KNEE CHAKRAS

People with blocked energy in the knee chakras may well be resistant to taking the next step. Physical manifestations might include swollen knees, soreness and "clicky," weak or stiff knees. There are acupuncture points located under the kneecaps, and there are also significant points at the backs of the knees: Weichung (equilibrium middle), the earth point on the bladder meridian, which has the effect of grounding fears, and Yinku (yin valley) on the kidney meridian, which gives an enormous boost to the water element and, therefore, courage.

1 Stand comfortably with your legs together. Make sure you have plenty of free space around you. First, transfer your weight to the left foot and kick out and shake the right knee to loosen it up. Then repeat for the other leg, transferring your weight to the right foot.

2 Stand with legs together, bend forward slightly and rub both knees vigorously, back and front, with your hands.

3 Next, keeping your legs together, hands on your knees, circle them nine times in one direction and then nine times in the opposite direction.

4 Stand upright and feel the increased circulation in your knees. Repeat a few times as you become more adept.

PALM OF THE HAND CHAKRAS

There is a chakra in the center of the palm of each hand, associated with a point on the circulation sex meridian, known as Lao Gong (palace of weariness). This fire point of a fire meridian revives an exhausted spirit, one that can no longer feel any joy—which is the emotion controlled by the fire element. It regulates chi, clears excess heat and stimulates a flagging sex life.

Healers use their own palm chakra to direct energy to their patients. It is actually quite easy to feel the energy in this chakra yourself, as you will discover if you do the simple exercise below. You already use it automatically whenever you rub a hurt, pat a friend on the back or hold hands with a lover.

1 Standing with your feet comfortably apart, rub your hands together vigorously.

2 Hold your hands out in front of you, about 2 feet (80 cm) apart and close your eyes.

3 Now move your hands slowly toward each other, and stop when you feel a resistance. This is your chi, or prana, projecting outward from the palm chakras. It often feels like an invisible balloon between your hands—enjoy playing with it. Try doing this exercise in the semi-dark and you may see your prana glowing.

HIP CHAKRAS

The gallbladder meridian runs through the hips and is associated with anger and with decision-making. Patients have been known to kick out when a healer works on treating this area, which can indicate physical or emotional abuse against them at some time in their lives. I have known patients who were repressing anger or struggling to make a decision manifesting hip problems such as sciatica, and showing mental inflexibility as well as physical.

1 Stand with your feet comfortably apart. Transfer weight onto your left foot, raise your arms to shoulder height and swing the left leg back and forward. Repeat five times and then do the same with the other leg.

2 Standing on your left foot, raise your right leg to the side five times. Repeat this on the other side.

3 Place your hands on your hips and circle them a few times in each direction.

DOOR OF INFANTS CHAKRA
Lower abdomen

There are acupuncture points on the kidney meridian near the surface of the body above where women's ovaries lie. Stimulating them can sometimes help women thought to be infertile to conceive, and it can also correct the functioning of the testes in men. Working on these points helps balance Svadisthana (see pages 32–9).

1 Lie on a mat in the relaxed position shown here and place your hands lightly over these points. Visualize a healing, orange light in this area. (If you are trying to conceive, send warmth and light to this area and imagine a door opening to your child.)

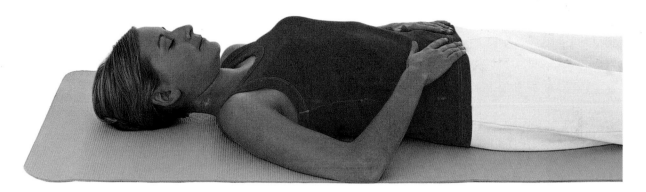

TAN TIEN CHAKRA
(Hara)

Two to three finger-widths below the navel is an extremely important energy store, like a reserve tank, known as the Tan Tien (pronounced "dan dien") in China, and the Hara in Japan. Although there is a series of acupuncture points along the midline from the navel down to the top of the pubic symphysis, I associate this chakra with Chihai (sea of chi). A pivotal center for balance on all levels, it encourages a sense of purpose and connects strongly to the solar plexus chakra, Manipura. When you need to feel physically steady (skiing, perhaps) or emotionally (when taking an examination), drop your attention to this point.

1 Stand with your legs hip-width apart, with your arms relaxed and by your side.

2 Bend your knees slightly and, keeping them bent, breathe into the Tan Tien and then back into the tailbone. Try to generate a sense of "dropping anchor."

SHENCHUEH CHAKRA
Exhausted spirit

In the center of the navel, Shenchueh (exhausted spirit) is so powerful it is forbidden to needle. However, it has the potential to retrieve someone from the depths of depression and is stimulated by burning cones of moxa herb placed on a belly button filled with salt, or on a slice of fresh ginger. It can revive the most exhausted spirits and bring them back from the brink, greatly supporting weak energy in Manipura.

1 Lie in a relaxed position with your left hand over your navel and your right hand resting on top. Visualize a golden light warming the navel area and spreading a glow in the back region.

MING MENG CHAKRA
Gate of life

Between the 2nd and 3rd lumbar vertebrae, Ming Men (gate of life) is where Manipura projects backward. Treating it is like placing a supportive hand on someone's back, helping them to move forward.

1 Stand with your feet comfortably apart. Make your hands into fists and massage the small of your back to warm it. Use just enough pressure to generate a warm glow in the treated area. Continue for a few minutes, or longer if you have the time.

SPLEEN CHAKRAS

These lie above the spleen on the ribcage. The spleen meridian controls the free movement of substances (such as blood and lymph) around the body, and our ability to get into action. Its peak functioning time is between 9 and 11 a.m.). It also helps us to express "si" appropriately, which is usually translated as sympathy. Signs that this chakra is weak might be fluids pooling in the body (varicose veins, swollen ankles) and an over-sympathetic or martyred nature, lack of sympathy, and hypochondria. The spleen chakras also affect sexual energy. It is not uncommon for a person who has weak spleen energy to stoop, having a somewhat deflated appearance.

1 Stand with your feet a comfortable distance apart. Place your hands over the spleen chakras, close your eyes and breathe a few deep yogic breaths into this area. As you do this, picture a golden light connecting down in a triangle to the sexual organs.

CHUNGWANG CHAKRA
Secondary solar plexus chakra

This chakra relates to the acupuncture point on the midline of the conception vessel meridian, known as Chungwang, and it is located roughly four finger-widths above the navel. It is a main center of energy, the meeting point for the five yang organs and the assembling point of the hollow organs. Keeping the energy in this area balanced helps the free-flowing expression of emotions, thus preventing any blockages and congestion.

1 Stand with your feet a comfortable distance apart. Close your eyes and breathe deeply into Chungwang (the secondary solar plexus chakra). While you do this, imagine the area vibrating with golden light and energy.

CHIMEN CHAKRA
Gate of hope

These liver meridian points nestle in the first "bay" of the ribcage, found by following the ribs up from the waist toward where the ribs meet. They are on a level just a little above the secondary solar plexus chakra. Helping us to express anger and to have foresight, a blockage here can result in deep depression. Treating them can literally revive hope and release anger.

1 Stand with your feet a comfortable distance apart. Follow your ribcage up from the waist with your fingers until they reach the first bay. Now gently massage the area with your fingertips. Then let your hands lie above the points for a few minutes and visualize a stream of green light coming from open doors beneath your hands.

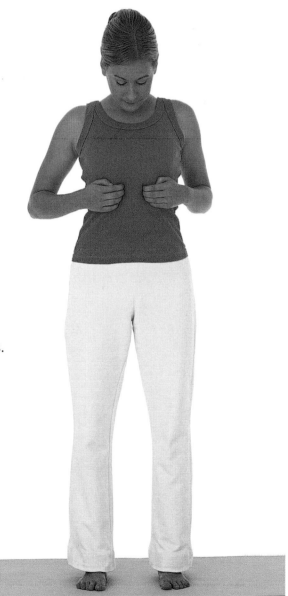

KALPAVRIKSHA CHAKRA
Kalpa tree

Known as the celestial wish-fulfilling tree, Kalpavriksha lies just above the heart chakra and can be said to be the subtler level of Anahata. The description of it in the old texts describes a luminous island of gems with a wonderful tree and a jeweled altar covered with an awning bedecked with flags. Said to grant our wishes, the paradox is that when it awakens, our heart's desire will be for the happiness and good of others. It can open only when Anahata has already done so, and I associate its opening with the final loosening of the vishnu granthi knot (see page 20).

1 Stand with your feet comfortably apart. Gently massage the area between the breasts or the center of your chest if a man, and just above the heart with your fingertips 21 times—clockwise for women, counterclockwise for men.

2 Rest your hand on this place, visualize the Kalpa tree, and send good wishes to all living things.

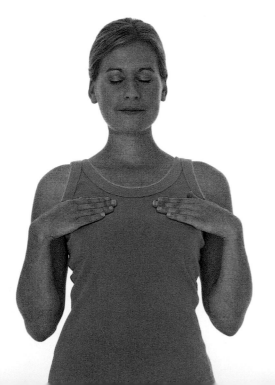

LINGHSU CHAKRA
Spirit burial ground

There are bilateral points on the kidney meridian on the chest just above the breast area (see page 77) known as spirit burial ground. Sometimes translated as "miraculous grove," they, too, can revive the spirit, bringing it back from the brink.

1 Stand with your feet comfortably apart and place your fingertips over these chakras. Visualize a blue healing light spinning beneath your fingertips penetrating deep into your chest and healing any emotional pain you are feeling.

THYMUS CHAKRA

The thymus chakra sits above Kalpavriksha in the center of the chest above the thymus gland. Most active in childhood, where its role is pivotal in the healthy functioning of the immune system, it tends to atrophy in adults. In former civilizations that were more spiritually attuned, it is thought that the thymus gland remained fully functioning. Another higher level heart chakra, we embody divine love here, and act from a truly compassionate nature. Physically it forms a link with the pituitary gland and generates energy.

1 Sit in a comfortable meditation position and close your eyes.

2 Breathe quietly, and picture someone, or somewhere in the world, where there is suffering. Visualize green/blue healing light pouring from your thymus chakra to that person or place.

3 Visualize the light growing stronger and stronger with each breath, and being replenished in a constant flow from the cosmos. End when you feel intuitively that the exercise is complete.

SHOULDERS CHAKRA

The chakras on the shoulder relate strongly to the metal element, to holding onto grief, regrets and the past. Poor posture with stooped or tense shoulders can indicate a block in these chakras. The associated meridians, colon and lung, pass through the shoulders. The left chakra relates more to karmic issues and the past, the right to the present. There is often an imbalance, with one functioning better than the other, creating symptoms on one side only. Sometimes re-establishing the flow of energy on the right shoulder inspires the patient with new ideas and enthusiasm.

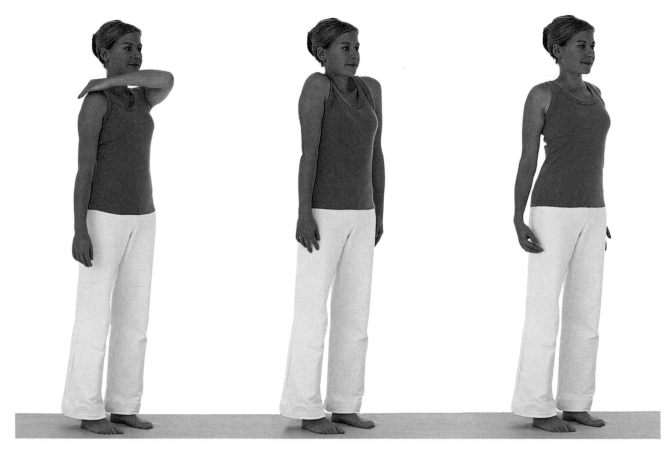

1 Stand with your feet a comfortable distance apart and pat each shoulder in turn. Pat up the side of your neck as well until you feel the circulation begin to tingle throughout your shoulders.

2 Next, rotate your shoulders forward, up, back and downward a few times, and then reverse the direction.

3 Now rotate your arms forward five times and backward five times, breathing in as you raise your arms, out as you lower them. Feel the glow in your shoulders when you have finished.

BACK OF THE THROAT CHAKRA

Being the backward projection of Vishuddha, this chakra has similar functions and associations (see pages 56–63). When the chakra starts to open it can sometimes cause discomfort and even pain. Energy here is often stronger in Taureans.

1 Sit comfortably cross-legged, inhale and then lower your head down until your chin presses against your chest, engaging the chin lock. Hold your breath for a few moments and then exhale. On your next inhalation, bring your head upright to release the chin lock. Another excellent exercise is shown on page 117.

LALANA AND BINDU VISHARGHA CHAKRAS

Lalana lies at the base of the nasal orifice and just above the throat. Bindu Vishargha is at the top of the brain, toward the back of the head (where Hindu monks keep a tuft of hair). These two chakras link in a triangle with Vishuddha. Sahasrara secretes drops of nectar that collect in the Bindu Vishargha (the name means "falling of drops"), which then drip from there to Vishuddha. When Vishuddha is awakened, these undergo purification and have the power to rejuvenate the entire body, and to give extraordinary powers of control over the body's metabolism. Yogis have been known to use these powers to survive being buried alive for 40 days.

Focusing on a triangle of light connecting Lalana, Bindu Vishargha and Vishuddha clears the head if you are tired and is also very refreshing for the sinuses.

1 Sit in a comfortable meditation posture and visualize a golden light connecting Vishuddha, Lalana and Bindu Vishargha. Picture the flow between the three points as you breathe quietly.

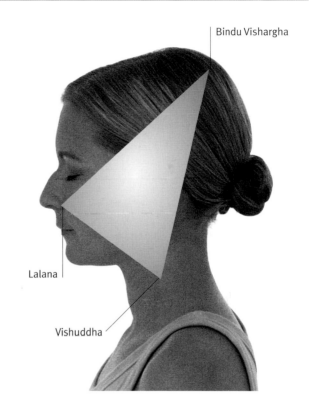

Bindu Vishargha

Lalana

Vishuddha

ALTA MAJOR CHAKRA

At the medulla oblongata at the back of the head, this chakra radiates the color magenta. It governs the carotid glands on either side of the neck, which control breathing, and therefore oxygen levels to the body.

1 Lie comfortably on a rug, close your eyes to exclude any room light and relax your whole body.

2 Now roll your head gently from side to side, visualizing a strong magenta light where your head touches the rug.

EYE CHAKRAS

One on each eye, these chakras are associated with sight, and with insight: the left eye with insights about the past; the right about the present. The eye exercises for Ajna chakra also balance these (see pages 118–19), as does the color indigo.

1 Sit in a comfortable meditation position. Close your eyes and breathe quietly.

2 Now rub your hands together vigorously and cup your hands over your eyes, cutting out all the light. Rest your eyes like this for a few moments, enjoying the inky darkness. Repeat this as many times as you like and then rest your hands on your knees, keeping your eyes closed all the time.

3 Next, visualize an indigo light bathing both eyes, bringing clarity and healing. Open your eyes when you feel you are ready. (You may notice a change in how you see things just after this exercise.)

SOMA CHAKRA

Soma means "nectar" or "the moon." This chakra is just above Ajna, the brow chakra, in the center of the forehead. It has a yantra of a silver crescent in a bluish-white lotus with 12 petals. This nurturing moon nectar (traditionally said to come from Kamadhenu, the wish-fulfilling cow) seeps constantly from the hollow space between the two hemispheres of the brain and flows downward to Manipura chakra, where it is burned up by the solar fire. Kamadhenu is a strange-looking creature—a white, horned cow with the face of a crow, human eyes, horse's neck, peacock's tail and the wings of a white swan.

Performing the khechari mudra (see below) stops the downward flow of the drops of nectar, and it is said to stem the aging process and bring eternal bliss. It allows the practitioner's mind to rest in the void, the space between the two hemispheres, known as the tenth gate of the body.

1 Sit in a comfortable meditation position and close your eyes.

2 Turn your tongue upward to touch the roof of your palate with the tip. Breathe quietly. This is khechari mudra.

SOUL STAR CHAKRA

Sometimes referred to as the 8th chakra, Soul Star is in alignment with Sahasrara, the 7th or crown chakra, but hovering above it. When it is fully open, this chakra links the person to the higher energies of the multiverse and to the soul. Much healing and guidance can come through to mind and body through this chakra.

1 Stand with your feet comfortably apart, arms open and palms facing forward.

2 Close your eyes and visualize a star 3 feet (1 m) or so above your head linking you to the multiverse.

4 | chakra asanas postures

Yoga is a science. The yoga postures, or asanas, work on the internal organs as well as on the musculature. People often ask why yoga makes you bend in all those peculiar positions. The answer is that apart from improving flexibility and circulation, the internal organs get a workout at the same time. The yoga positions treat the organs something like sponges, compressing them, and when they are released they receive an inrush of well-oxygenated blood from the good breathing that accompanies the postures (see Using pranayama, page 92). The entire body is rejuvenated, including the nervous system.

Did you ever help stretch sheets, tugging them crosswise to straighten them? Most of the stretches that follow help to align the body, and keep the skeletal system strong and upright. The postures help the chakras to communicate by aligning the spine and keeping it that way with strong supportive musculature. You would not lay a communication cable deliberately putting kinks in it. The spine, which carries the subtle energy of the Sushumna right up the middle, needs to be straight for Kundalini to rise, and for those energies to flow freely up and down. Picture the old people you know. I bet that the ones with masses of energy are the ones with straight spines.

The tendons and ligaments can be visualized like the guy ropes of a tent. When a tent flops over in one direction, you tighten the guy ropes on the other side to bring it upright again. The body is the same. When people develop poor posture through stress or lifestyle, they need to realign their body by adjusting the guy ropes (tendons and ligaments) and may need to work temporarily more in one direction than another.

Before you start yoga, it helps to take a long, hard look in a mirror at your relaxed, naked body. Do your shoulders slump or are they held tense around your ears? Do you have a distended belly, with tightness in the small of your back (see box right)? Are your calf muscles shortened by constantly wearing high heels?

Habitual posture problems

If a muscle is tight (the dark tone shows the shortened chest muscles of person A) you need to stretch it more and contract the opposing muscles (pale tones). If these muscles are not corrected, as soon as you relax you will sink back into poor posture. Eventually you must work in a balanced way, but you may need to do more forward bends, for instance, and avoid back bends until you are straight, if you look like person B.

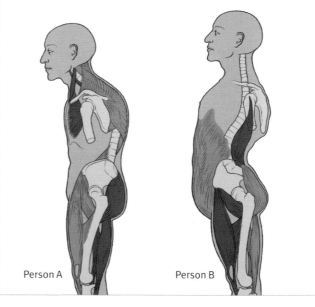

Person A   Person B

a word about asanas

While it is always better to learn the postures, or asanas, from a properly qualified yoga teacher, there are steps you can take when learning them from a book that will greatly ease the whole process.

When you first try the asanas, see if you can find a friend who will read out the instructions to you as you try the poses to make sure you are doing them correctly. Alternatively, any good yoga class will include the postures in this book, or ones very similar—you can imagine stimulating the relevant chakra as you do the asanas there. Indeed, including visualization adds depth and focus to any yoga practice, so that even an experienced yogi benefits from the most basic class. It is one of the signs of truly evolved yogis that they never complain about doing the simple postures, nor do they feel the need to compete by showing off.

I have included a warm-up sequence at the beginning of this section, which I strongly recommend you do not omit, especially if you are living in a cooler climate. It may seem unnecessary when you are in a hurry, but in fact the warm-ups stimulate the minor chakras, which is why they make you feel so good.

As I have mentioned previously, physical release is a requirement for the seven main chakras to open. The warm-ups increase the circulation generally, improve your breathing, warm the ligaments and tendons, improve flexibility in the postures and fluidity in the joints, thus making your practice much easier and safer. So beneficial are they that if you are really pressed for time on a particular morning, they could substitute for the postures, as long as you do them in a yogic frame of mind and with focus.

Yogis say that you are as young as your spine. But in order for the spine to achieve maximum flexibility you need to move it in all the directions it is capable of moving. So when you choose asanas to perform, select a combination that flexes the spine forward, bends it backward, rotates it and flexes it sideways. The general

rule of thumb is that when you have moved the spine in one direction you counterpose by moving it in the other direction immediately afterward—for example, follow a forward-bending posture with a backward-bending one; if you bend to one side, also bend to the other. Follow this advice unless you have a medical reason not to, such as sciatica.

Where to practice

All you need is a level floor area, somewhere draft-free, where you will be warm, comfortable and undisturbed. Yoga on a quiet beach in the sunshine can hardly be bettered or, if you prefer, on a sunny lawn or under the shade of a tree. It's best to use a mat or a rug—these days, "sticky" yoga mats that protect you from slipping are available. Make sure you have enough room to stretch out your arms and legs in all directions without banging into obstructions and restricting your asanas. Having said that, I have often thought of writing a book on "tent" yoga … yoga that needs very little space. It helps to set the scene with candles, incense and fresh flowers— whatever promotes a quiet, focused frame of mind.

When to practice

Choose a time that will not compromise digestion: in other words, no less than two hours after a light meal or a minimum of four hours after a full meal. It's impossible to do the asanas properly or comfortably on a full stomach. First thing in the morning before breakfast is a very good time to practice them, and they will set you up for the day, improving metabolism, circulation and digestion and giving you clarity of mind.

If you practice last thing at night, choose poses—such as the Five Tibetans—that don't stimulate you too much.

When not to practice

When you are ill (with the flu or something similar) it is best to allow the body to rest—it may be ideal for you to do what I call "sleep yoga" to recover. Women who are menstruating are usually advised to avoid the inverted asanas, but often find that the other postures help alleviate cramps. People with high blood pressure should avoid asanas that take the head below the level of their heart. It is always best to be safe, so if you have any form of medical condition that you are uncertain how yoga will affect, check with your doctor before starting.

Although at one time many doctors generally were suspicious of yoga, most now recognize its benefits to their patients and will most likely encourage you to do it if at all possible. Wheelchair users can do many of the warm-ups as well as some of the poses, but they may need someone to assist them and to adapt poses.

Age limit

There really is no age limit to practicing yoga—but of course it is best to start young. I was impressed by my very first yoga class when a couple in their 80s walked nearly 1 mile (2 km) to class, and back, and did all the poses with the rest of us every week without fail. It was a good lesson: improved flexibility is possible at any age. Use it or lose it!

Using pranayama

While asanas have the power to control the physical body, pranayama (*prana* = breath, *yama* = control) controls the subtle, astral body, the linga-sarira, and the nervous system (see pages 12–15). Yogis consciously learn to combine asana and pranayama. First, you need to become familiar with the postures, without worrying too much about getting the breathing right, and then gradually add pranayama. When you first begin, take an extra breath whenever you need to and try to remain relaxed about the whole process. Before long, you will find that correct breathing with the postures becomes second nature. It brings an entirely new dimension to your practice and you will feel greatly increased benefits—and experience the power of true yoga/union.

A general rule is that the opening movements in the postures—lifting the arms, for example, or arching the back—usually require an inhalation: *puraka*. Closing movements—such as forward bends or lowering arms— usually use an exhalation: *rechaka*. A retained breath, in or out, is known as *kumbhaka*. Holding an inhalation allows more time for the uptake of oxygen by the lungs and is energizing; holding an exhalation is calming. Most postures use the yogic complete breath. Imagine that you are filling your lungs as if a bottle, down to the bottom first. This should make your abdomen rise; when you breathe out it contracts. A full yoga breath moves like a wave, filling the bottom of the lungs, expanding the chest, lastly moving right up to the collarbones. On breathing out, the diaphragm relaxes up toward the lungs, making the abdomen contract, and requires no effort at all—it will just happen naturally. Watch the way babies breathe—they usually get it right! Full details of pranayama are included in the next chapter.

You might choose to perform the posture to the rhythm of one complete breath, inhaling as you move into position, holding the inhalation while you hold the posture, exhaling as you come out of the posture. The ultimate aim is gradually to extend the time you hold a posture, using an inhalation to get into the posture, then maintaining quiet yogic breathing while you hold it, and coming out of the posture inhaling and then exhaling as you move. There are exceptions, as in the Five Tibetans (see pages 124–8), but they are unusual.

The right attitude

Finally, it's important to stress the importance of having the right attitude to your yoga practice. Setting the scene before it starts is part of this, with a warm, comfortable space where you won't be disturbed.

You need a certain amount of dedication in order to maintain regular yoga practice, but you will reap the reward if you do stick at it. You will get out of yoga benefits in the exact proportion of the effort you put in. Yoga is one of the greatest treats you can give yourself, and will help you to enjoy good health on all levels throughout your life.

warm-ups

Don't worry about any clicking or cracking noises you hear as you warm up—people often mistake this for bones crunching, but it is merely the fluid "popping" in the joints as it becomes more viscous, and is completely harmless. Take a moment to pause after each movement to feel the difference between the joint you have worked and the other side.

FEET

Our feet literally ground us. These movements activate the earthy base chakra and minor chakras on the feet.

1 Stand on a non-slip yoga mat with your feet a comfortable hip-width apart. Transfer your weight to the left foot and give your right foot a good shake. Then do the same with your left foot.

2 Rise up onto the balls of your feet while breathing in, and lower your heels while breathing out. Repeat this three times.

3 Walk forward a few paces on the outsides of your feet, and back on the insides.

ANKLES

As we work the ankles we activate six meridians: bladder, kidney, gallbladder, stomach, liver and spleen.

KNEES

The knees carry inappropriately withheld/expressed anger. These exercises work on the minor knee chakras to correct this problem.

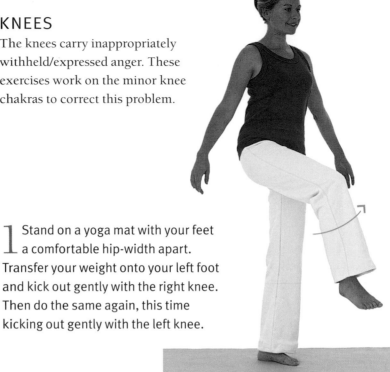

1 Stand on a yoga mat with your feet a comfortable hip-width apart. Transfer your weight onto your left foot and kick out gently with the right knee. Then do the same again, this time kicking out gently with the left knee.

1 Stand on a yoga mat with your feet a comfortable hip-width apart. Transfer your weight onto your left foot and circle the right foot five times in one direction, five times in the other.

2 Now, with your weight transferred to the right foot, do the same with your left foot.

2 Rotate your lower leg five times in one direction and five times in the other. Then do the same with your left leg.

HIPS

The hips also hold anger. Moving them in this way smoothes our moods and makes us less inflexible.

1 Stand on a yoga mat with your feet a comfortable hip-width apart. Transfer your weight onto your left foot, raise your arms to shoulder level and swing your right leg backward and forward, leading with your heel so that the leg swings like a pendulum. Repeat this five times and then do the same with the other leg.

2 Transfer your weight onto your left foot and raise your right leg out to the side five times (being careful not to tilt to the left). Then do the same on the other side.

3 Put your hands on your hips and circle them in an almond shape, a few times in each direction.

WAIST AND RIBCAGE

These movements allow the spine to rotate in a perfectly balanced way.

1 Stand with your legs wider than hip-width apart, sink onto a slightly bent right knee and turn to face your left leg. The toes on that foot should be raised, stretching the back of the leg, and let your arms swing around your body.

2 Now transfer your weight over to the other side, letting your arms swing around your body, and do the same on the other side. Get a rhythm going, right and left, and feel the rotation in the spine and stretch around the waist.

SHOULDERS

Our shoulders often hold onto inappropriately expressed/withheld grief. Rotations help to release this.

1 Stand with your feet a comfortable hip-width apart and circle your shoulders a few times in one direction, and then a few times in the other direction.

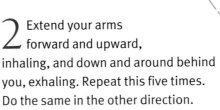

2 Extend your arms forward and upward, inhaling, and down and around behind you, exhaling. Repeat this five times. Do the same in the other direction.

NECK

Pause in the center between each movement to let the tendons realign. Repeat each three times in total.

1 Standing or sitting comfortably, breathe in as you lower your head forward. Breathe out as you lower it toward your chest. As you breathe in, come back to the upright.

2 Lower your head gently back by slightly tilting your chin up (this should not be an extreme movement). Breathe out as you lower it and in as you come back to the upright.

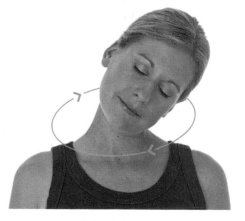

3 Lower your right ear down toward your right shoulder, and then your left ear down toward your left shoulder. Keep the same breathing pattern as in step 2.

4 Breathe in and out as you turn to look over your right shoulder. Keep the back of your neck lengthened and your chin on an even, horizontal axis. Breathe in as you bring your head back to the center. Repeat in the other direction.

5 Circle your head around three times in one direction, three times in the other, being careful not to tilt the neck back too far. This is more of an almond-shaped movement than a circle.

muladhara gateway of earth

Muladhara chakra governs our sense of security and relates to the earth element. Located in the perineum, postures that focus energy here activate it. They are particularly helpful at times when we feel anxious.

VAJRASANA
The thunderbolt

All the sitting postures stimulate Muladhara, the first chakra, but the static Vajrasana pose is very beneficial. Being so simple, it is a good one to start with. Vajrasana brings peace and serenity to practitioners, grounding them to the earth like a thunderbolt and making them feel safe and secure. It is a good asana, or posture, to use for resting between exercises.

1 Sit on your yoga mat in a kneeling position, legs hip-width apart, buttocks on your heels.

BENEFITS

❖ Stimulates Muladhara, making you feel secure and peaceful.
❖ Improves posture, aligning the spine correctly.
❖ Stretches the quadriceps.

PRECAUTION

❖ If you have varicose veins you may feel more comfortable with a cushion or blanket between your calves and thighs.

2 Rest your hands comfortably on your thighs and lengthen the back of your neck by tucking in your chin. Close your eyes, or lower your gaze to look at a point on the floor 3 feet (1 m) or so in front of you, and take a few deep yogic breaths (see pranayama on pages 137–43).

3 Rest quietly in this pose, breathing quietly, feeling contact with the ground and say to yourself: "I am secure and the Earth supports me." Contract and hold and then relax the muscles around your anus three times—this is mula bandha, the anal lock (see page 19). Imagine a red light projecting from Muladhara down into the center of the planet.

BODY DROPS

The movement in this posture greatly improves the circulation to the perineum and, therefore, to the base chakra, stimulating it.

1 Sit upright on your yoga mat with your legs stretched out in front of you, feet together.

2 Place the palms of your hands on the mat 12 inches (30 cm) or so behind your buttocks and slightly out to the side.

3 Repeatedly lift and drop your buttocks a few inches from the mat, breathing normally as you do so. Stop when your arms feel tired.

BENEFITS

❖ Promotes a strong sense of security.
❖ Gives a good stretch to the spine.
❖ Massages the inner organs.
❖ Rejuvenates the entire body.
❖ Stimulates Muladhara chakra.

PRECAUTION

❖ Don't take your head below the level of your heart if you have high blood pressure. Make two fists of your hands, placed one above the other, and rest your head on them.

GARBHASANA
Child pose

This is a very comforting asana to do, taking us right back to our early months in the womb.

1 Kneel in the thunderbolt pose (see page 98), with your hands on your thighs and legs hip-width apart.

2 Breathe in and exhale, bending forward from the hips to rest your upper body on your thighs. At the same time, take your arms backward alongside your body, palms up. Rest your forehead on the mat (see Precaution above).

3 Breathe deeply, feeling the movement of your ribcage on your thighs, and completely relax in the pose for as long as you are comfortable.

4 Slowly return to the upright pose in step 1 when you are feeling relaxed and ready.

svadisthana gateway of the moon

Svadisthana governs creativity, on both the physical and emotional levels. Postures that activate it by focusing on the pelvic basin where it is located stimulate creativity and help to balance emotional and sexual needs.

BHUJANGASANA
The cobra

This posture helps to regulate the function of the uterus and gonads, and works strongly on Svadisthana. It also helps to realign the spine if it is out of line.

BENEFITS

❖ Regulates the gonads and uterus.
❖ Improves circulation to the pelvis.
❖ Realigns the spine.
❖ Strengthens the upper back.

PRECAUTIONS

❖ Don't do this pose if you are pregnant.
❖ Beginners may prefer to repeat the exercise without holding the pose.
❖ Counterpose with the child pose (see left).

1 Lie on your abdomen and relax, stretching out your legs. Place your forehead on the mat, and your hands palms down with your fingertips in line with your shoulders (or eyes if you are a beginner).

2 Inhale, lengthen the back of your neck, exhale and raise your forehead, nose, chin, shoulders and upper back and chest in a snakelike movement. Use your arms just for balance; make your back do the work. Keep your hips in contact with the mat. Hold the pose with quiet breathing for a few moments. Visualize an orange light in the pelvis and say to yourself: "I open to my creativity."

3 Exhale, slowly uncurling your spine, lowering your chest, chin and nose until your forehead rests on the mat. Lengthen the neck and repeat three times.

DEVIASANA
Goddess pose

This pose opens the pelvic region like a flower, and brings focus to Svadisthana. Imagine an orange glow in that region as you do the exercise. The preparation for it is extremely good for the lower back—often implicated when there are blocks to creativity or sexuality.

1 Lie on your back on the mat, bend your knees and keep them and your feet together (feet close to your buttocks), arms by your side, palms down.

BENEFITS

❖ Improves circulation to the pelvis.
❖ Stretches the inner thigh muscles.
❖ Prepares the body for cross-legged poses.
❖ Brings flexibility to the lower back.
❖ Soothes period pain.
❖ Stimulates Svadisthana.

PRECAUTION

❖ It may help to put blankets or support under where your knees will reach until the pelvis fully opens to the floor.

2 Take a breath in and press the small of your back into the mat, breathing out as you do so. At the same time, allow your pelvis to tilt and lift off the mat slightly. Then, breathing in, relax your back onto the mat, allowing the slight curve in the back to return. This forms a rocking movement, which you can repeat until you feel the area loosen up.

3 Next, take your arms out from the body a little, palms down. Inhale and lower your right knee down to the mat as far as is comfortable, exhaling and keeping your feet together, opening out the pelvis. Inhale, bringing the knee back up and repeat on the other side, three times each side in total. You should feel a comfortable massage to the base of the spine and lower back.

4 Finally, lower both knees to the floor at the same time and relax with the pelvis open, soles of the feet together, breathing deeply into that area. Imagine an orange glow in the pelvis getting stronger with each breath. As you lie in the pose say to yourself: "I open to my creativity." Enjoy relaxing this way until you feel ready to come out of the pose.

SHALABASANA
The locust

This posture puts pressure on the pelvic region and stimulates Svadisthana. It also mobilizes the lower back and strengthens it.

1 Lie face down on the mat, legs together, chin on the mat, arms by your side and hands tucked under your thighs palms up.

BENEFITS

❖ Greatly strengthens the lower back.
❖ Tones the legs and buttocks.
❖ Improves circulation to the pelvis.
❖ Stimulates Svadisthana.

PRECAUTIONS

❖ Your chin should not lift off the floor.
❖ Keep your hips down on the mat.
❖ Counterpose with a forward bend, such as the child pose (see page 100).

2 Inhaling, point your toes and raise your right leg. Use your fingers to help, lifting it as high as you can without bending it or taking your hip off the floor. Lower when you are ready to exhale, tying the movement to the breath.

3 Inhaling, point the toes of your left foot and lift
your left leg as high as you can. Repeat this three
times, alternately lifting your right and left legs.

4 Now, inhaling, raise both legs together and hold the pose
for a few moments if possible, breathing quietly. When
you are ready to come down, breathe in and then exhale as you
return to the start position. As you hold the pose say to yourself:
"Each moment brings opportunity for creativity." Repeat this
three times.

manipura gateway of the sun

Manipura is our power center. When we do postures that focus on the abdominal area where it is located, we balance the way that we express personal power, giving us quiet confidence.

UDDIYANA BANDHA
Abdominal lift

Uddiyana tones the abdomen and stimulates Manipura. It is also very comforting to do when you are feeling a little nauseous. It is one of the three main locks, or bandhas, that focus energy in Kundalini (see pages 18–19). Come out of the posture with control before you feel as if you will burst.

BENEFITS

❖ Tones the abdomen.
❖ Massages and lifts the abdominal organs.
❖ Helps to reduce nausea.
❖ Stimulates Manipura.

PRECAUTIONS

❖ Don't do this asana if you are pregnant.
❖ Don't hold your breath until the bursting point.

1 Stand with your feet just a little wider than hip-width apart and bend forward slightly, resting your hands on your thighs. Bend your knees slightly.

2 Breathe in deeply and then exhale thoroughly. Now pull your abdomen in, up and back toward your spine so that it forms a hollow. Keep your lungs empty and hold for as long as possible.

3 Come out of the pose when you are ready, returning to an upright position, inhaling and then exhaling long and slow. Repeat three times.

PASCHIMA NAUASANA
The boat

The boat generates a strong contraction to the abdomen and, therefore, a concentration of energy in Manipura. It is a powerful posture, emphasizing that quality generated by the chakra. It also works strongly on the meridians that control fear and anxiety (see also the bridge, page 108). It is a balance posture, which promotes this sense emotionally.

BENEFITS

❖ Provides a strong emphasis to Manipura chakra.
❖ Tones the abdomen, legs and arms.
❖ Works on the bladder and kidney meridians, which help control fear.
❖ Works on the stomach and spleen meridians, which balance sympathy and anxiety levels, and help us to be appropriately assertive.
❖ Tones the inner organs.
❖ Improves digestion.
❖ Promotes an inner sense of calm, balance and power.

PRECAUTIONS

❖ If you have back problems, do this asana one leg at a time, other knee bent up.
❖ Always use the abdominal muscles to lift yourself into this pose, not the back.
❖ Don't arch your back.
❖ Counterpose with the bridge posture.

1 Lie on your mat and fully stretch out. Keeping your arms by your sides, hands palm down and legs together, breathe in deeply. As you breathe out, raise both legs and trunk at the same time, using only your abdominal muscles (to protect your back). At the same time, raise your arms until your hands are level with your knees. Hold the point of balance with quiet breathing. Keep your head facing forward and your gaze steady to the front and imagine a golden light at the abdomen. Feel strong and steady, say to yourself: "Nothing rocks my boat."

2 Come out of the posture in reverse order, inhaling a deep breath and exhaling it as you lower.

SETU BANDHA
The bridge

This posture brings a wonderful stretch to the abdomen, opening up the Manipura area. It contracts the kidneys and stretches the bladder meridian, helping you to feel more confident while, at the same time, strengthening the back. There is also a strong stretch to the stomach and spleen meridians in the earth element, which rule digestion, our ability to feel sympathy, anxiety, to feel balanced and be appropriately assertive (see page 24–31). The contraction on the throat regulates the thyroid gland, so there is also benefit to the hormonal system.

BENEFITS

- ❖ Works on the kidney and bladder meridians, increasing confidence.
- ❖ Works on stomach and spleen meridians, controlling anxiety, improving digestion and helping us to be appropriately assertive.
- ❖ Balances the hormone system.
- ❖ Greatly improves flexibility and the strength of the spine.
- ❖ Improves flexibility of the shoulders if you use the arms.
- ❖ Increases strength in the legs.
- ❖ Tones legs and buttocks.
- ❖ Relieves tension in the neck.
- ❖ Releases the emotions.

PRECAUTIONS

- ❖ Make sure your feet don't slip by keeping them close to your buttocks.
- ❖ If you are holding the posture, keep breathing quietly and evenly.
- ❖ Warm up the back before starting (see goddess pose, page 102).
- ❖ Counterpose by holding your shins, drawing your knees in toward your chest, and your forehead toward your knees.

1 Lie on a non-slip yoga mat (barefoot is safer) and bend up your knees, placing your feet hip-width apart about 18 inches (45 cm) from your buttocks. Tuck your chin in slightly to extend the back of your neck and place your arms by your sides, palms down.

2 Exhale thoroughly, then inhale as you tilt your pelvis, pressing the natural curve of your spine into the mat. Then peel your spine off the mat, vertebra by vertebra from the tailbone, until your hips are raised right off the mat and your chin is tucked into your chest in the chin lock, jalandhara bandha (see page 19). Your breath should be timed with the movement.

3 You can make the posture stronger by taking your arms up over your head and down to the floor behind you as you come up, but to time them to arrive with the full extension of the back they will have to move faster, making it a good concentration exercise. Breathe quietly if you are holding the pose and visualize a golden light at your abdomen. Say to yourself: "I am strong and appropriately powerful."

4 When your are ready to come down, inhale, and exhale as you lower your spine (and arms if you raised them) onto the mat from your neck down to your tail, vertebra by vertebra, just as if you are wallpapering and don't want to trap any bubbles. Again, the movement should be timed with the breath. Repeat from the start three times.

anahata gateway of the winds

Anahata chakra, which governs how we express compassion and love, can be activated and balanced by postures that literally open the heart. All these postures expand the chest area.

ANGEL WINGS

This posture opens the chest and flexes the upper back. It works strongly on the heart chakra and, therefore, on your ability to feel compassion, an attribute you tend to associate with angels. Visualize a green light projecting out from between your breasts, or the center of your chest, as you do this moving sequence.

BENEFITS

❖ Tones and stretches the chest and upper back.
❖ Improves posture.
❖ Opens the heart chakra.

PRECAUTIONS

❖ None.

1 Stand tall with the back of your neck lengthened and your feet hip-width apart. Inhale and stretch out your arms at shoulder height, palms facing forward.

2 Exhale and, with your next inhalation, stretch your arms backward without bending the elbows as if you were trying to make your shoulder blades meet. Lift up your chin and raise your chest upward and outward. Say to yourself: "My love is expansive."

3 Exhale, bringing your arms around to the front, hands touching, and curve your upper back slightly forward.

4 Repeat the full movement several times—arms back with the inhalation, forward with the exhalation—finishing with an exhalation as you slowly lower your arms.

BENEFITS

❖ Opens the heart chakra area and works on Anahata.

❖ Provides a strong stretch to the ribcage and legs, improving flexibility and releasing blocks on the gallbladder and liver meridians, thus releasing anger.

❖ This is one of the few postures that promote sideways flexibility of the spine.

❖ The strong compression it provides on the abdomen aids elimination and so can relieve constipation.

❖ Works on the colon and lung meridians, releasing resentments.

❖ Opens the hips.

❖ Builds stamina.

❖ Promotes flexibility of the mind.

❖ Trims the waist.

PRECAUTIONS

❖ While this posture can cure sciatica (where the nerve is trapped by the spine), you should stretch only the painful side—contracting it will make it worse.

❖ It is very important to keep the hips square to the front, or the posture will turn into a forward bend instead of a side bend and lose the intended benefits.

❖ It is important always to go down to the right first, compressing the right side of the colon first in order to aid elimination.

TRIKONASANA
The triangle

So often our ability to feel compassion is blocked by anger. The triangle, apart from giving a strong stretch to the chest area and, therefore, Anahata, also gives a good stretch to the meridians that control anger: the gallbladder and liver. Thus, the pose helps us have a more balanced point of view and to feel compassion. It brings flexibility to the spine, and the mind tends to follow. The strong compression on the colon helps to rid us of resentments, which is another block to feeling compassion.

1 Stand with your legs far enough apart to give them a stretch without any painful straining. Keep your feet facing forward, heels in line. You are aiming to create an equidistant triangle: in other words, the space between your legs should ultimately be the same as the length of your legs.

2 Inhaling, turn both feet toward the right, but keep your hips square to the front (in the manner of an Egyptian frieze). Exhale.

3 Keeping feet and hips in the same position, inhale, raising your arms sideways to shoulder height, palms facing downward.

4 Exhaling, bend from the waist down to the right, letting the right arm stretch down and lightly touch your right leg. The left arm stays in line with the shoulders and reaches up to the ceiling, palm turned to face the front. Look up at your left hand if you can do so without strain. Breathe quietly if you are holding the posture. Say to yourself: "I open to compassion."

5 When you are ready to come back up, use an inhalation to help you return to the start position. Exhale as you lower your arms. Repeat three times in the same direction. Release the legs, give them a shake and then repeat the posture three times on the left.

GOMUKHASANA
Head of the cow

This strong posture really opens the chest and, therefore, Anahata chakra. It works hard on the arms as well as the chest muscles, giving a good stretch to the heart meridian and to its protector, the pericardium meridian. Both help us to feel and share joy appropriately.

BENEFITS

❖ Opens Anahata chakra.
❖ Improves flexibility in the shoulder area.
❖ Helps to cure round shoulders.

PRECAUTIONS

❖ Don't arch your back to make the hands meet.
❖ Keep your neck lengthened, chin tucked slightly in.
❖ Always perform some shoulder rotations after this asana.

1 Sit in Vajrasana, the thunderbolt (see page 98). Breathe in and lift up the right arm and place your right hand as far as you can between your shoulder blades. Then breathe out.

2 Now breathe in and take your left arm around behind you and bend it so that your left hand reaches up between the shoulder blades. Breathe out.

3 Breathe in and try to clasp your right hand with your left. Then breathe normally. Face forward and imagine a green light projecting out from your heart to other people. Say to yourself: "My heart is open." (If your hands don't meet, you can hold a sock or a handkerchief in your upper hand and grasp that with the lower hand. In time your hands should meet.)

4 Unwind when you are ready to come out of the pose and rotate your shoulders a few times. Then rest with your hands on your thighs. Reverse the pose on the other side.

Vishuddha gateway of time and space

The warm-up exercises for the neck (see page 97) are also excellent at stimulating the throat chakra. They may be executed on their own as one of the Vishuddha exercises. If you use them in this way, visualize turquoise light emanating forward from your throat as you do the movements.

JALANDHARA BANDHA
Chin lock

The third of the three bandhas, which focus energy in the Sushumna to raise Kundalini energy (see pages 18–19), is the chin lock, which also works strongly on Vishuddha chakra. It is often used in conjunction with breathing techniques (see pages 137–43) and in some postures (see the bridge pose, page 108).

BENEFITS

❖ Focuses energy in Vishuddha chakra.
❖ Keeps energy in the Sushumna, helping to raise Kundalini.
❖ Frees up a stiff neck.

PRECAUTION

❖ Do not hold your breath too long or you will become dizzy.

1 Sit in an easy, cross-legged pose (see the easy pose, page 147).

2 Inhale and then lower your head down until your chin presses against your chest, creating the chin lock. Hold your breath for a few moments (kumbhaka) before exhaling.

3 When you are ready to inhale, release the chin lock and bring the head back up to an upright position.

SIMHASANA
Lion pose

This pose is highly beneficial if you have a sore throat. Whenever you suffer this way, ask yourself: "What am I avoiding saying to someone?" You can feel the energy in the throat chakra after doing the lion pose, and you will be encouraged to speak your mind more clearly and from a deeper level if you have previously been timid about expressing yourself. (Communication on this level is usually well received.) The second version, with the roaring and crossed eyes, goes over particularly well with children.

BENEFITS

❖ Brings energy to Vishuddha chakra.
❖ Helps to cure a sore throat.
❖ Helps to get rid of phlegm.
❖ Promotes clear communication.

PRECAUTION

❖ Make adjustments according to the length of your arms and legs. Come up onto your fingertips if necessary (it will strengthen them).

1 Sit in Vajrasana (see page 98), the thunderbolt, with your knees hip-width apart.

2 Kneel forward and sit back on your heels with the weight on your hands in front of your knees and on the balls of your feet.

3 **Version One** Stick out your tongue as far as possible, cross your eyes and focus on a point between your brows. Exhale and draw in your stomach muscles, as in uddiyana bandha (see page 106). Tense your entire body.
Version Two Stick out your tongue as far as possible and cross your eyes as before, but this time roar loudly as well. Tense your entire body.

4 **Both Versions** Relax and inhale when you are ready and rest back in the thunderbolt, feet flat, for a few moments. Breathe normally. Repeat three times.

MATSYASANA
The fish

Matsyasana stretches the throat chakra like no other asana. While you do it, imagine turquoise light radiating forward from your throat.

BENEFITS

- ❖ Stimulates Vishuddha chakra.
- ❖ Improves posture.
- ❖ Deters wrinkles.
- ❖ Benefits the thyroid gland.

PRECAUTIONS

- ❖ Use a cushion under the head if you feel uncomfortable going back so far.
- ❖ Always counterpose at the end by lifting your head off the mat to look at your feet.

1 Sit on the mat, with your legs together straight out in front of you. Lean back, putting one elbow on the mat, then the other.

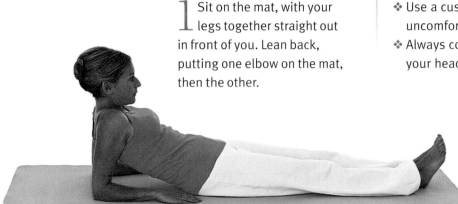

2 Breathe in, arch your back and lower the crown of the head onto the floor (use a cushion if necessary). Take your hands up into prayer position if you can. Hold this for a few moments breathing quietly. Make the affirmation: "I trust my inner voice, and speak the truth clearly."

3 If you are comfortable taking it to the next stage, arch your back a little more, taking your elbows off the mat, or hands from prayer position, and rest your hands on your thighs. Hold for a count of ten if you are comfortable, quietly breathing.

ajna gateway of liberation

Ajna chakra, which is located in the forehead, is our center of intuition. Since it also rules the eyes, and foresight, exercising them as described below will stimulate it, as will chanting Om.

NETHRA VYAYAMAM
Eye exercises

Often neglected in yoga practice, these eye exercises are very important, not only because they stimulate Ajna chakra, which rules the eyes, but also the two minor chakras (one on each eye—see page 77).

BENEFITS

❖ Stimulates Ajna chakra.
❖ Can improve eyesight.
❖ Strengthens the muscles around the eyes.
❖ Improves circulation to the eyes.

PRECAUTION

❖ If you wear hard contact lenses you may need to take them out before performing these exercises.

1 Sit in a comfortable cross-legged position, left heel into the inner thigh, right heel in front, with your buttocks supported by a cushion or block. Rub both palms together vigorously and cup your hands over your closed eyes for a few moments. Enjoy the soothing, inky darkness.

2 Gradually open your fingers to allow light in. Then open your eyes and lower your hands.

3 Imagine you are sitting in front of a large town hall clock. Look up to the 12 o'clock position and down to the 6 o'clock position five times. Squeeze and relax your eyes tight shut a few times.

4 Now do the same, looking from the 3 to the 9 o'clock position five times. Then squeeze your eyes tight shut a few times.

5 Next, look from the 1 to the 7 o'clock position five times. Squeeze your eyes as before a few times.

8 Focus on a point in the far distance and then at one 3 feet (1 m) or so in front of you five times. Say to yourself: "I honor and value my insights."

9 Finish with the cupping exercise described in step 1.

6 Look from the 11 to the 5 o'clock position five times, and then squeeze your eyes a few times.

7 Now go right around the clock from 12, clockwise, pausing at each number. Do the same counterclockwise. Squeeze your eyes a few times.

CHANTING OM

Though not an asana, chanting Om stimulates Ajna, so it is appropriate to include it here. The mantra has many meanings: the sound of all sounds, the beginning of life, the sound of creation. When we chant Om we in fact go through four stages—ahh, uh, mmm (Aum) and silence.

1 Sit in a comfortable position with your back straight somewhere you won't be disturbed.

2 Inhale deeply and chant Om, going through the first three stages with the exhalation.

3 After the pause for silence repeat the chant, and do this several times more.

4 Sit relaxed and absorb the silence for a few moments afterward.

BENEFITS

❖ Enhances energy in Ajna chakra.
❖ Brings about a sense of peace.
❖ It is a powerful spiritual exercise.
❖ Dispels negativity.
❖ It fills you with radiance.

PRECAUTIONS

❖ None.

sahasrara gateway of the void

Sahasrara chakra, where we open to unity and bliss, is on the crown. It is stimulated by postures that intensify energy here. Safer than the headstand, try the half and full shoulderstand (see pages 122–3), or the hare (below).

SASANGASANA
The hare

The hare is an excellent posture for Sahasrara and has the benefit of being easier on the neck than the headstand, which also benefits Sahasrara, but is best learned from a teacher.

BENEFITS

- ❖ Helps to activate Sahasrara.
- ❖ Reverses the force of gravity.
- ❖ Improves the complexion.
- ❖ Brings freshly oxygenated blood to the brain, pituitary and thyroid glands.

PRECAUTIONS

- ❖ Never take your head below the level of your heart if you have high blood pressure. This pose is not for you.
- ❖ Check first with your doctor/osteopath if you have a weak neck.
- ❖ Always take time to rest in the child pose for a few moments to finish (see page 100).

1 Start in the child pose (see page 100), and then place your hands on the mat either side of your knees.

2 Inhale, lifting your buttocks up and transferring weight to the crown of your head (see Precautions). Exhale.

3 Inhale as you clasp your hands behind your back and raise them as high as you can, feeling the contraction between your shoulder blades. Exhale then breathe quietly holding the pose for as long as is comfortable. Visualize a mauve light on the crown of your head and repeat the affirmation: "I am open to the multiverse. There are no limitations."

4 When you are ready, exhale back down to the child pose. Rest there for a few minutes, breathing quietly, before you sit up.

BENEFITS

❖ Enhances energy in Sahasrara.
❖ Regulates the sex glands, poor blood circulation and menstrual and seminal problems.
❖ Relieves varicose veins temporarily; helps piles temporarily.
❖ Reduces abdominal fat.
❖ Relieves dyspepsia and constipation.
❖ Has been claimed to help cure asthma, liver and intestinal disorders.
❖ **Note:** Whole books have been written about the benefits of Sarvangasana— these are just a few of them.

PRECAUTIONS

❖ Don't try this pose if you have high blood pressure.
❖ Check with your doctor/osteopath if you have neck problems.
❖ Never turn your neck when you are in the pose.
❖ Come down immediately if you feel a sneeze or a cough coming on.
❖ Counterpose by leaning back on your elbows and taking your head back, or by adopting the fish pose (see page 117).

SARVANGASANA
Half or full shoulderstand

Another safe alternative to the full headstand to balance Sahasrara is the half or full shoulderstand. *Sarva-anga-asana* means beneficial pose for the whole body. It tones the most important thyroid gland.

1 Lie on a non-slip mat, legs together and arms down by your side. Bend your knees up and rock back and forth a few times to loosen up. When you are ready, roll up with your legs balanced at a 45° angle over your head. Support your back with your hands. Hold this position with quiet breathing and focus on Sahasrara, picturing a violet light at the crown of your head. Continue to the next stage or straight to step 3.

2 If you feel able to, take the asana to the next stage. Straighten up your back so that it is vertical, at a right angle to your neck, with your chin locked into your chest. Move your hands higher up your back to support this position, and keep your elbows in. Imagine a plumb line hanging vertically from your toes. Breathe quietly in the pose, toes pointed, until you feel ready to come down. (Beginners should not hold the position—rather, repeat it three times instead.)

3 Come out of the pose by bending your knees toward your forehead and slowly rolling down, using your outstretched arms along the floor to balance and support you.

five tibetans rites of rejuvenation

There are two sequences (posture flows) that work strongly to balance energy in all the chakras—the sun sequence, known as Surya Namaskar, and the Five Tibetans. The first is very well known and is taught in most good yoga classes, is illustrated in charts, on T-shirts and in many yoga books. In this book I present the less well known and intriguingly mysterious Five Tibetans. For anyone undertaking serious work on the chakras it is a must, extremely powerful, and can stand alone as an early-morning sequence whenever you are pushed for time.

The story of the Five Tibetans begins with a retired British army officer who learned five specific exercises from Tibetan lamas in a Himalayan monastery. He passed these on to author Peter Kelder, who published a book entitled *The Five Rites of Rejuvenation* in 1939. In the book he describes the exercises, claiming that they bring amazing powers of rejuvenation, strength and an increase of energy to body, mind and spirit—and that they stem the aging process. In 1994, Christopher Kilham wrote a book renaming the exercises the Five Tibetans, and adding the pranayama that I use here.

From my own experience I cannot praise this set of exercises more highly for all the claims listed above, except for the last—ask me again in 20 years! What I can say is that practicing these asanas early every morning has made me more supple at 57 than I was at 30. The days when I practice this routine always seem to go with a "zing," my mind is clear, the writing flows and I have energy in abundance throughout the day.

Start with five repeats and over the weeks increase to a maximum of 21. Note that the breath is the opposite of normal—inhaling with a folding movement—and I believe that it is this that concentrates the energy in the Sushumna, the body's principal nadi, or meridian, that connects all the chakras (see page 16). You may prefer to use the more usual pranayama, exhaling when you fold.

BENEFITS

The following beneficial points apply to all the Five Tibetans:
❖ Tones the entire body.
❖ Stimulates all the chakras, including the minor chakras.
❖ Strengthens the back.
❖ Promotes core strength.
❖ Improves communication between the seven main chakras.
❖ Stimulates the circulation.
❖ Loosens joints and promotes flexibility.

For Tibetan No. 5 only:
❖ Strengthens and tones the back, arms and wrists.
❖ Reduces excess fat in the abdominal area.

TIBETAN NO. 1
Spinning

❖ You may experience dizziness initially. Start slowly as advised, and focus on the leading hand. In time the vestibular apparatus controlling balance in the inner ear is strengthened by whirling.

1 Stand erect and raise your arms to shoulder level, palms facing downward. Start to turn, pivoting on the balls of the feet.

2 Turn clockwise five times. Do this slowly when you first begin, in case you become dizzy, and gradually increase the speed over the weeks until it is a spin—like a Whirling Dervish. (It helps to keep your eyes focused on your leading hand to counter feelings of dizziness.) Finish by taking two deep, yogic breaths, exhaling through the mouth, lips pursed, hands by your sides and feet together.

TIBETAN NO. 2
Leg raising

❖ If you have a back problem, do this exercise one leg at a time.

1 Lie on a non-slip mat with your feet together, palms flat by your sides, and inhale while raising both legs just past 90°. Stretch the back of your legs by extending your heels up. At the same time, lift your head up, tucking your chin into your chest. Keep your lower back flat so that it is supported on the mat.

2 When you are ready, come down slowly, exhaling, to the start position, head and legs working together. Repeat five times and then take two deep yogic breaths.

TIBETAN NO. 3
Back arch

❖ If you suffer from lordosis (sway back), do not increase the repeats beyond five.
❖ Take your head back only as far as is comfortable for you.

1 Kneel up on your mat and tuck your toes under, knees hip-width apart. Keep your arms relaxed by your sides, spine erect and chin tucked into your chest.

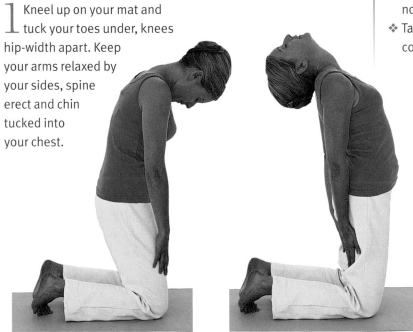

2 Inhale and arch backward, taking your head back only as far as you can without straining, and place your hands below your buttocks for support. (Some people prefer to keep facing the front.)

3 Exhale, returning to the start position, and then repeat five times. End with two deep breaths.

TIBETAN NO. 4
Belly push

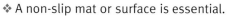

PRECAUTIONS

❖ A non-slip mat or surface is essential.
❖ Hands can face forward or backward.
❖ If you have short arms you might need to use blocks or fingertips. Don't curve your back for your arms to reach.

1 Sit upright, legs outstretched in front of you, toes up, and place the palms of your hands on the mat exactly beside your hips. Then, tuck your chin into the chest.

2 Inhale and push your hips up, bending your knees, soles of your feet flat on the mat. Your head should go back as far as is comfortable for you. Your thighs, trunk, head and neck form a a flat, tablelike surface.

3 When you are ready, exhale returning to the original position. Repeat five times. Finish the sequence by taking two deep, yogic breaths.

TIBETAN NO. 5
Dog/raised cobra

❖ A non-slip surface is essential.
❖ Unlike most inverted triangle poses, here you must keep the heels raised.

1 Start by lying on your front and then supporting your weight on your palms and the balls of your feet. Keep your head up and slightly back.

2 Inhale as you push your buttocks up, staying on your toes, and take your head toward your knees between your arms. Keep your chin tucked in to form a perfect triangle.

3 Exhale returning to the start position. Repeat five times, then sit back on your heels and take two deep, yogic breaths.

Maha mudra

Maha is Sanskrit for "great." This posture is of great benefit both physically and spiritually, and works strongly on all the chakras.

1 Sit on your mat with legs outstretched in front of you. Bend your left leg and tuck the heel into your inner thigh, against the bone of the perineum, so that it presses into it. If you are a man, make sure that your genitals do not get in the way. The sole of your left foot should be in close contact with your right thigh.

2 Bend over enough to take hold of your right foot with both hands, just below your toes, keeping the foot vertical.

BENEFITS

❖ Awakens the central nervous system and produces massive brain wave activity.
❖ Greatly stimulates energy in Sushumna.
❖ Balances and energizes all the chakras.

PRECAUTIONS

❖ Always perform this on an empty stomach.
❖ Don't hold your breath to the point of dizziness.

3 Breathe in and, retaining the breath (kumbhakha), perform the anal, abdominal and chin locks—the mula, uddiyana and jalandhara bandhas (see page 19).

4 Relax the bandhas, breathe out with control and sit up.

5 Stretch out your legs and repeat on the other side.

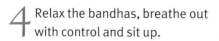

5 | pranayama breath control

The softest thing in the universe
Overcomes the hardest thing in the universe.
—*Tao Te Ching*, Lao Tzu

For nine months we wait in the protected world of the womb while that most miraculous of systems, our body, develops. When our time comes, we struggle into the world, inflate our lungs, and cry the first breath. And we keep on inflating and deflating our lungs, around 23,000 times a day, for what might be 80 years or more.

The vital force

Yogis place the highest importance on correct breathing and breath control. They understand that with each intake of oxygen, there is another substance taken into the lungs—prana, a Sanskrit term meaning "absolute energy," the vital life force. Found in all forms of life, prana is all pervading. It is in every atom, even in apparently lifeless things, permeating the multiverse. There is a sample of jade in the Science Museum in London that has become smooth with the stroking hands of visitors. Place your hand on the stone and you feel it vibrate with prana.

This energy force is at its most abundant on mountain tops, under trees, by moving water—especially waterfalls and the sea. People are drawn to these places to recharge on vacation. We also recharge our prana with good food and drink, sleep, uplifting work and good company.

A person with abundant prana has a glow, a radiance that makes them very attractive. The Chinese call this shen, or spirit. Increasing the flow of prana improves energy levels; correcting its flow can prolong life and cure many diseases. This is why exercises such as yoga or tai chi, and treatments such as acupuncture or ayurvedic medicine, which balance prana/chi, are so effective. Prana nourishes the nervous system in the same way as oxygen nourishes the circulatory system.

In the description of Svadisthana chakra (pages 32–9) I spoke of the birth of ideas. Using breath consciously to strengthen intention before we act, and as we act, makes it far more effective. But be careful where you place your attention. Prana follows the direction of the mind. We need to be wary of wasting prana by directing it into resentful or negative thoughts. Others receive our thoughts, good and bad. And remember the old adage of being careful what you ask for.

Modern life depletes prana. Food is denatured, irradiated, microwaved, reheated and may have traveled halfway around the world and be almost devoid of prana by the time it reaches your plate. Sleep prana, or jiva, is lost to late-night television and a social or work life that continues into the small hours with the aid of electric light. People smoke and pollute their lungs with noxious poisons. Prana is also depleted by an excess of emotions, even the "good" ones—think of the pressure to be highly sexually active. Modern living with little family support and scant connection to nature cannot restore the balance, nor can two weeks on a beach.

Conserving prana

So how do we increase our prana? In the last chapter I described how to use breath with the postures, but stressed the importance of getting the posture right first. This is because correct posture is a prerequisite for the successful practice of pranayama. The two can be learned concurrently, it is just a question of emphasis. Correct breathing with the postures will develop as you practice.

In the following pages I describe the mechanics of breathing and the most common techniques used by the yogis. Pranayama is particularly relevant because it is almost impossible to make any significant spiritual progress without it. While some techniques are very good for certain chakras, all the techniques benefit all of the chakras. It is best to learn one thoroughly until you become adept, and then move on to the next one.

the mechanics of breathing

Most newborns breathe correctly. Over the years, tensions in the body and in our lives affect the correct mechanics. Diaphragms get tense and work less effectively, poor posture restricts the chest. Yogic breathing can correct this, but it is helpful to understand the basic mechanics of breathing first.

Think of your lungs as an inverted tree. The main trunk is the trachea, or windpipe, kept open by rings of cartilage. The windpipe divides into a pair of large, major branches, the bronchi, which, in turn, divide many times into smaller and smaller branches, eventually forming extremely fine branches, known as bronchioles. The bronchioles open into clusters of thin-walled sacs called alveoli.

The lungs are spongy, porous and elastic. They are contained in, and protected by, the pleural sac, one wall of which attaches to the lungs, the other to the inner wall of the chest. There are three lobes on the right side of the body, and two on the left (leaving room for the heart). The lungs are free except at their root, where they connect with the trachea, and at the heart, where they connect to the pericardium that sheaths it. Each time you breathe your heart receives a gentle massage.

Before air enters the trachea it passes through the nose, where it is filtered for impurities by fine hairs. It then passes over the turbinates, which act like radiator baffles, where it is warmed and moistened. Next it passes over the pharynx and the larynx (Adam's apple), which is responsible for the voice and guarding the airway against the entry of food or liquids.

Suckling babies breathe on average about 50 times a minute, a young child between 15 and 25 times and adults between 10 and 14 times a minute. A man's lungs hold roughly 1½ gallons of air and a woman's about 1 gallon. During normal resting respiration, approximately 1 pint of air is taken into the lungs. However, a deep yogic breath can take in as much as 1¼ gallons, and so clears the stagnant air that usually sits in the bottom of the alveoli.

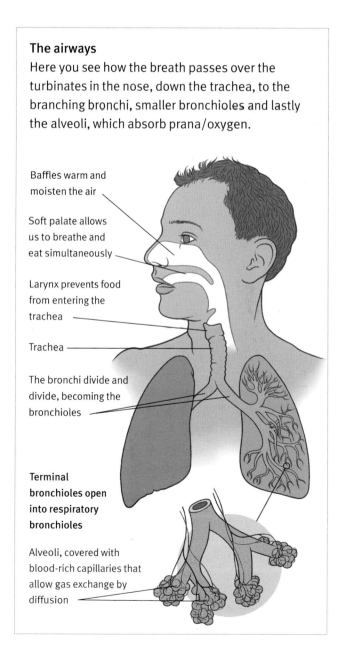

The airways
Here you see how the breath passes over the turbinates in the nose, down the trachea, to the branching bronchi, smaller bronchioles and lastly the alveoli, which absorb prana/oxygen.

Baffles warm and moisten the air

Soft palate allows us to breathe and eat simultaneously

Larynx prevents food from entering the trachea

Trachea

The bronchi divide and divide, becoming the bronchioles

Terminal bronchioles open into respiratory bronchioles

Alveoli, covered with blood-rich capillaries that allow gas exchange by diffusion

Conscious and unconscious breathing

Messages in the respiratory center in the brain stem about the levels of CO_2 in our blood control breathing without any conscious effort on our part. But the depth and rate of breathing can be altered voluntarily, and this is pranayama. You already practice pranayama when you swim or exert yourself physically in some other way, blow up balloons, play a wind instrument, or blow out the candles on your birthday cake.

Puraka, kumbhaka and rechaka

When we inhale, air is drawn into the lungs by the action of the intercostal (chest) muscles found between the ribs, which cause the ribs to rise like the handle on a bucket. The diaphragm, which is a large, dome-shaped muscle when relaxed, contracts and flattens down toward the abdominal organs with the intake of breath—this is why you see the abdomen expand when a person is breathing in correctly. The action of the ribs and diaphragm increases the volume in the chest cavity, thus creating a partial vacuum and causing the lungs to expand and suck in air. This is known as puraka. Holding an inhalation allows more time for the blood to absorb oxygen and so boost energy levels. Many pranayama techniques involve retaining an inhalation. The pause with retained breath is known as kumbhaka.

What makes us breathe?

The diaphragm acts like a plunger (below left), creating a vacuum as it contracts, drawing air into the lungs for an inhalation. The lungs stretch and inflate to fill the entire thoracic cavity, as shown in the cutout illustration (below right). The diaphragm relaxes up toward the lungs in a dome shape, forcing air out of the lungs for an exhalation, and re-creating the vacuum ready for the next intake of air.

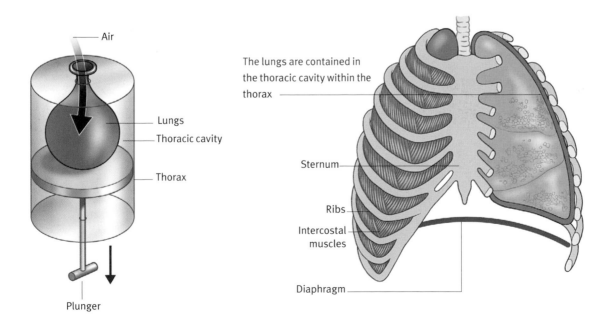

Air

Lungs

Thoracic cavity

Thorax

Plunger

The lungs are contained in the thoracic cavity within the thorax

Sternum

Ribs

Intercostal muscles

Diaphragm

When you exhale, the intercostal muscles relax, the ribcage falls, and the diaphragm relaxes back into its characteristic dome shape up toward the lungs and heart, and so air is expelled from the lungs. This is known as rechaka. When there is a pause with the lungs deflated (also known as kumbhaka), there is less oxygen absorption, more CO_2 in the blood and a calming effect.

Blood circulation

The thin walls of the alveoli in the lungs allow the interchange of stale air, charged with carbon dioxide, with freshly oxygenated air, via tiny blood-filled capillaries. Approximately 70 percent of all the waste elimination in the body is managed in just this fashion, so it comes as no surprise that people find that taking a good walk in the fresh air, getting the lungs pumping, is invigorating and puts roses in their cheeks.

The left side of the heart pumps oxygenated blood into the major arteries, which distribute it via the blood vessels and capillaries to every cell in the body. Blood takes up carbon dioxide in the process and carries it back to the right side of the heart via the veins. Venus blood is darker red than freshly oxygenated blood. The right side of the heart then pumps deoxygenated blood from the body tissues into the pulmonary artery where it is carried to the lungs to be reoxygenated.

How we breathe
These illustrations show how the diaphragm contracts downward (below left) toward the stomach and lower abdominal organs when we inhale, and then relaxes up (below right) toward the lungs when we exhale.

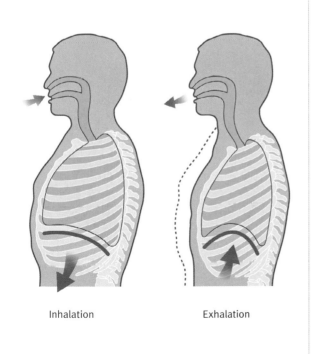

Inhalation   Exhalation

Breathing and circulation
Bright red, oxygenated blood passes from the lungs to the left ventricle of the heart, which pumps it to every cell in the body. Blue, deoxygenated venus blood is returned to the right ventricle, where it is pumped to the lungs for reoxygenation.

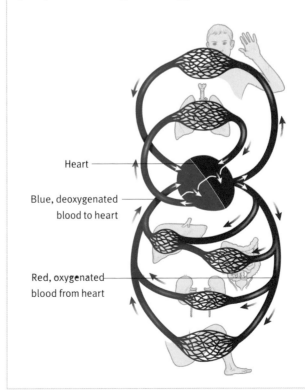

Heart

Blue, deoxygenated blood to heart

Red, oxygenated blood from heart

the metal element

The ancient Chinese observed nature closely, and noticed how it is reflected in the human organism, identifying a correlation between the organs and their related meridians, and the five elements. For a full understanding of how the lungs work we need to understand how they relate to their element: metal.

The lung and colon meridians are said to be in the metal element. The metal element is analogous to the precious stones and minerals that are found within the rocks and mountains of the Earth. This is a reference to the spiritual dimension that these meridians and, particularly, the lungs, bring to our lives. They inspire—literally and metaphorically. There is a link with our relationship to our father, earthly and heavenly. Many people with breathing or associated lung problems have a difficult or, paradoxically, exceptionally close relationship to their fathers, and may be searching for the spiritual dimension that they feel is lacking in their lives.

On the physical level, the metal element controls elimination; psychologically it controls grief. The color associated with an imbalance in the metal element is white. People who have a problem with their lungs (and also their colon) display a white coloration around their eyes and mouth, and this sometimes spreads to their whole face. They also have a quivering or weeping tone to the voice. Anyone who has lung and breathing problems, such as asthma or bronchitis, will greatly benefit from practicing the breath control that stems from pranayama.

Some benefits of correct breathing
- Flexible spine
- Improved posture
- Correct movement
- Healthy nervous system
- Improved circulation
- Increased vitality
- Powerful, sweet, melodious voice
- Regular, thorough elimination
- Healthy immune system
- Well-oxygenated blood
- Improved metabolism
- Well-regulated autonomic system
- Balanced pH

Some symptoms of incorrect breathing
- Bad posture
- Contracted chest
- Stooping
- Restricted movements
- Nervous tension
- Anxiety
- Poor circulation
- Asthma, bronchitis, pleurisy and so on
- Susceptibility to many infections
- Fatigue
- Weak voice
- Resentment
- Inappropriate grief
- Depression

areas of expansion

It is helpful to identify and isolate the various areas of the chest and abdomen that expand during a yogic complete breath. When you are comfortable breathing in each individual area they can be put together in sequence to form the complete breath.

ABDOMINAL/LOW BREATHING

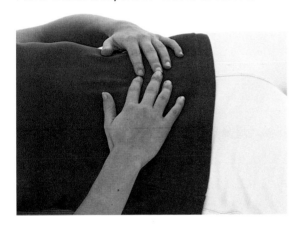

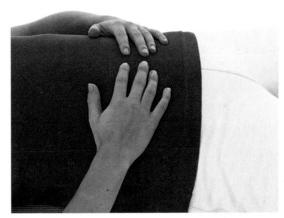

1 Lie on your yoga mat for a few moments and have a good stretch. Then rest both hands lightly on your belly, over your navel, with your middle fingers just touching.

2 Keeping your chest still, breathe into the lower lobes of the lungs. Imagine that you are filling a bottle with water, pouring the water (in this case air) down to the bottom of the bottle. Notice how your fingers part as your abdomen expands when the diaphragm goes down, and relax back together once more as you exhale.

3 Keep this up for a few minutes, using a steady count: breathe in to a count of four; hold for a count of four; breathe out for a count of four; and hold your lungs deflated for a count of four. You can use your heartbeat to time the counts if you like. Adjust the count to one that suits you if you feel uncomfortable.

RIB/MID BREATHING

1 Sit upright in a comfortable position and bend your arms, placing your hands on either side of your ribcage. Breathe out completely.

2 Inhale into the middle of your chest, feeling your ribs expand up and outward to a count of four, hold the breath in for four, exhale for four and hold out for four. Keep this rhythm going for a few breaths until you feel really comfortable with it and can feel your ribcage expand.

3 Now place the backs of your hands on the middle of your back. Repeat the breathing exercise so that you can feel your chest is expanding backward, too.

UPPER CHEST/HIGH BREATHING

1 Sitting in a comfortable position, place your hand lightly on your upper chest, just below the clavicles.

2 Breathe lightly, a maximum of five breaths, into the upper chest. Feel the very minimal expansion that is possible in this area. It is very important that you do no more than this. Breathing into this area tends to make us feel anxious.

basic pranayama techniques

Once you have identified the areas of expansion, you are ready to try the following techniques. If any of these exercises make you feel dizzy, or cause you any problems, it is best to get help learning them from a properly qualified yoga teacher. If you have high blood pressure, consult with your doctor first, and show them the method as described.

UJJAYI
Sounding breath

One way to control your breath is by using the small flap of flesh at the back of the soft palate. This is the muscle that you use involuntarily when you snore and voluntarily when you gargle. It's like directing the flow of water from a hose by partly closing the end with your thumb. By partially closing the windpipe with this flap as you breathe in and out, you have more control over your breath. Try it now with an ordinary breath. You will find it makes a slight pre-snoring sound. Mastering this technique makes the long, slow, measured breaths much easier.

Ujjayi is a particularly good technique to practice for the throat chakra—Vishuddha—since it vibrates the vocal cords, placing your attention firmly there, and because the associated sense is hearing.

BENEFITS

❖ Expels stale air from the lungs and purifies the respiratory system.
❖ Balances the emotions.
❖ Calms the nervous system.
❖ Relaxes the body.

PRECAUTION

❖ This exercise should not make you feel dizzy. Stop at once if it does.

1 Sit in a comfortable position and place your hands lightly on your knees.

2 Exhale completely, deflating your lungs as far as you can.

3 Breathe in slowly to a count of six through your nose, feeling the abdomen, ribs and chest expand, partially closing off the throat with the flap, so that you make a humming sound.

4 Close the flap totally while you hold the breath in for a count of six.

5 Breathe out slowly to a count of twelve, flap half closed, so that the exhalation is equally controlled, making a slight hissing sound.

6 Hold your out breath with your lungs deflated for a count of six. (You can adjust the count to suit, using the same proportions.)

7 Repeat this sequence for a few breaths initially, and then gradually extend the period to five or ten minutes as you become more adept and comfortable with the procedure.

THE COMPLETE BREATH

There is a common misconception that with yogic breathing low, or belly, breathing is best. In fact, though that is good for identifying how the diaphragm works, and exercising it when it has long been held rigid, correct breathing includes all three areas, and is known as the complete breath. It brings into play the entire respiratory system and generates maximum benefit. It is the breath used most commonly while performing asanas, and should become second nature in time as your normal breathing pattern—of course, you won't be taking in a full volume of air during normal, quiet breathing, but the movement should be as described.

When you first try this technique, it may feel as if it divides into three distinct movements, but soon you will find that the components flow easily into each other. You can do it lying, sitting, while performing the asanas or, indeed, at any time to a greater or lesser degree.

BENEFITS

❖ Fully utilizes all the breathing muscles.
❖ Encourages the maximum expansion of the lungs.
❖ Leaves you feeling energized and balanced.
❖ Improves your general posture.
❖ Helps to remove stale air from the bottom of the lungs.

PRECAUTION

❖ Stop at any time if you feel dizzy, and change the count to one that suits you better if you feel any undue strain.

1 Lie on a mat and have a good stretch. Your arms should be by your side but slightly out from your body, palms up. Your feet should be relaxed, 18–24 inches (45–80 cm) apart. Breathe out completely.

2 Using the three areas of expansion (see pages 135–6), in sequence like a wave coming into the body, begin by breathing in deeply to the bottom of your lungs, contracting the diaphragm down for a count of two.

3 Continue the breath into the mid part of your chest for a further count of two.

4 Finish the inhalation by breathing in to the upper chest region for the last count of two.

5 Hold your breath in for a count of six, with your chest and ribs fully expanded—your abdomen will have pulled in slightly to achieve this.

6 Relax and breathe out, not worrying about the order—the exhalation will manage itself—to a count of eight.

7 Hold the breath out, with your lungs deflated, for a count of six.

8 Repeat the whole sequence as described here for several minutes, until the waves of breath feel completely natural and require little conscious control.

BENEFITS

❖ Cleanses and tones the respiratory system and nasal passages.
❖ Removes spasm in bronchial tubes (some asthmatics claim to have been cured).
❖ Develops lung capacity.
❖ Increases oxygen absorption.
❖ Removes impurities in the blood.
❖ Increases energy.
❖ Warms the body.
❖ Improves concentration.
❖ Tones the circulatory system.

PRECAUTION

❖ Stop if this exercise make you feel dizzy.

KAPALABHATI
Breath of fire

Kapala is the Sanskrit word for "skull"; bhati means "to shine." I take this to mean that it has a strong effect on the crown chakra, Sahasrara (see pages 70–5), and it has the effect of improving concentration. Because it uses the abdominal muscles very strongly, it works particularly well on Manipura, the solar plexus chakra. Warming and energizing, kapalabhati is one of the six cleansing exercises of hatha yoga, purifying and oxygenating the entire system. You may find that you sweat profusely during this exercise.

1 Sit in a comfortable cross-legged position and rest your hands on your knees. Make sure that your body remains upright throughout this practice, and lower your chin. Breathe out thoroughly, emptying your lungs.

2 Close your eyes and inhale slowly, but exhale rapidly and vigorously. The exhalations should be more pronounced than the inhalations, and they should be done quickly and forcibly by contracting the abdominal muscles with a backward push. The inhalation should be mild, slow and long.

3 To begin the sequence, do approximately one expulsion of breath per second, gradually building to two per second.

4 Start with one round in the morning, breathing ten times in and ten times out.

5 In the second week, increase the frequency of the exercise by adding an additional round in the evening.

6 In the third week, do two rounds in the morning and two rounds in the evening.

7 Gradually increase the number of inhalations and expulsions until you are doing 120 per round.

BHASTRIKA
Bellows breath

Once you have become adept at kapalabhati (see page 139) you should find Bhastrika very easy. Bhastrika means bellows. This technique features a rapid succession of forced expulsions of breath, much as a blacksmith would pump his bellows. It even makes a kind of wheezing sound like bellows. Each round is completed with a long, deep inhalation, held for as long as comfortable, and a long, slow exhalation. Bhastrika is a powerful exercise. It actually constitutes a combination of kapalabhati and ujjayi, so it is best learned after you become comfortable doing them.

Bhastrika has the power to release the three knots—the brahma, vishnu and rudra granthis (see page 20)—and the "bolt on the door of the Sushumna." Therefore, it is excellent for raising Kundalini (see page 18) and should take pride of place in working on the chakras. Physically it is said to destroy diseases arising from wind, bile and phlegm, to warm the body and purify the nadis.

BENEFITS

❖ Warms the body.
❖ Relieves inflammation of the throat.
❖ Improves digestion and increases metabolism.
❖ Destroys phlegm.
❖ Can cure asthma and other respiratory diseases.
❖ Purifies the nadis/meridians.
❖ Releases the three granthis, or knots.
❖ Raises Kundalini.
❖ Benefits the liver and gallbladder.
❖ Strengthens the lungs.

PRECAUTION

❖ Stop if this exercise makes you feel dizzy.

1 Sit in a comfortable, cross-legged pose with your hands on your knees. Keep your trunk erect and head and neck in line with your spine, chin lowered. Breathe out fully and close your mouth.

2 Inhale and exhale very quickly ten times, pumping your lungs like the bellows of a blacksmith. You should make a hissing or wheezing sound as you do this.

3 Inhale deeply a complete breath and hold it for as long as is comfortable.

4 Exhale as long and slowly as possible. This is the completion of one round.

5 Rest for a while, taking a few normal breaths, before repeating the exercise.

6 Complete three rounds daily in the morning and another three rounds in the evening.

SITKARI
Thirst-quenching/cooling breath

Sitkari means to have or to possess. *Sit* in Sanskrit also means cold. Thus, Sitkari is a pranayama that cools. The sound "sit" is made while you do the exercise. Physically it is very cooling to the eyes and soothing to the ears. It is a help in lowering a mild fever. It also stimulates the spleen and liver, improves digestion and temporarily relieves thirst if you find yourself in a situation where you cannot drink.

BENEFITS

❖ Produces a cooling effect.
❖ Refreshing, especially if you are thirsty.
❖ Soothes the eyes and ears.
❖ Relieves biliousness and mild fever.
❖ Stimulates the liver and spleen.
❖ Improves digestion.

PRECAUTION

❖ Stop if this exercise make you feel dizzy.

1 Sit in a comfortable, cross-legged position, or back on your heels, with your hands resting on your knees. Breathe out thoroughly.

2 Open your mouth slightly and place your tongue behind your upper incisors. The sides of your tongue should cover your lower molars and premolars.

3 Open your lower jaw, allowing your tongue to press lightly between the upper and lower molars. The padding of your tongue will leave a small opening between your front teeth.

4 Suck in air through this small opening, making the sound "si."

5 Close your mouth after the inhalation. This will make the sound "t."

6 Hold the breath in for four times the length of the inhalation.

7 After this time, with your mouth still closed, breathe out evenly through your nose.

8 Continue, following these steps, for a few rounds.

SITALI
Cooling breath

As with Sitkari (see page 141), the name of this breath relates to its cooling effect. Normally, breath is warmed and moistened in the nose. Here, the breath is drawn in through a tube made by curling your tongue to produce a cooling effect. (Don't worry if you can't make a complete tube—just do the best you can.) It is best not to practice sitali where the air is exceptionally cold or hot.

BENEFITS

❖ Produces a cooling effect.
❖ Soothing to the eyes and ears.
❖ Relieves the symptoms of mild biliousness and fever.
❖ Improves digestion.
❖ Improves metabolic system.
❖ Activates the liver.

PRECAUTION

❖ People with high blood pressure should practice this exercise initially without retaining the breath.

1 Sit in a comfortable, cross-legged position, or back on your heels, with your hands resting on your knees. Breathe out thoroughly.

2 Stick out your tongue about ½ inch (1.5 cm) from your lips and fold up its edges so that it forms a tube.

3 Inhale slowly through the opening at the front of the tube.

4 Close your mouth and hold the breath in for four times longer than the inhalation.

5 Breathe out slowly through your nostrils. This completes one round.

6 Start with five rounds of sitali and gradually increase to 15.

7 When you are adept at this you can add in the bandhas (see page 19) to the kumbhaka, or held breath (see page 132).

ANULOMA VILOMA
Alternate nostril breath

This is one of the most powerful and beneficial of yogic breathing techniques. You will find that practicing it makes you feel exceptionally calm and clear, for it soothes and purifies the central nervous system. Besides this, it helps you to develop control of your mind and emotions, clears the nose and normalizes metabolism. Normally we breathe mainly through one nostril for 10 to 15 minutes, and then change to the other. There follows a period of 10 to 15 minutes when we breathe evenly through both nostrils. When we breathe predominantly through the right nostril we activate left-brain function and are in the mood for action. Left-nostril breathing stimulates right-brain function and promotes a quieter, more reflective mood. The ancient yogis would use the appropriate nostril for the task in hand. When we breathe evenly through both nostrils we are calm and balanced—the end result of anuloma viloma. It is a very beneficial exercise to use before exams, interviews or any situations you might find stressful.

1 Blow your nose thoroughly before starting. Sit in a comfortable sitting position, back straight.

2 Using your right hand, rest the index and middle fingers in the center of the forehead. Breathe out thoroughly.

3 Slowly inhale through both nostrils, then close the right nostril with your thumb.

4 Breathe out through the left nostril.

5 Breathe in through the left nostril.

6 Close the left nostril with your ring finger, release the thumb, and breathe out through the right nostril.

BENEFITS

❖ Balances the nervous system.
❖ Clears the nasal passages.
❖ Increases concentration and alertness.
❖ Relieves stress.

PRECAUTION

❖ Stop if this exercise make you feel dizzy.

7 Breathe in through the right nostril, close it with your thumb, breathe out through the left nostril, and so on. Keep up an even rhythm.

8 As you become more comfortable with the rhythm you can change the ratio, making the exhalation longer and slower. Start doing this for five minutes at a time, gradually increasing until you can comfortably practice alternate nostril breath for up to 20 minutes.

6 | dhyana meditation

… that serene and blessed mood,
In which … the breath of this corporeal frame,
And even the motion of our human blood,
Almost suspended, we are laid asleep
In body, and become a living soul:
While with an eye made quiet by the power
Of harmony, and the deep power of joy,
We see into the life of things.
—*Tintern Abbey*, William Wordsworth

Why meditate?

Meditation, or dhyana, is the penultimate step on Patanjali's eightfold path (see page 21), taking us toward the deeper reason to practice yoga: samadhi, meaning bliss or self-realization. Having said that, it is best to meditate without expectation, for there are many benefits before samadhi and, ironically, one of the blocks to successful mediation is to practice with an attitude of expectation. It helps to cultivate a passive attitude, and avoid what Wordsworth called "little enemies and low desires."

We deceive ourselves that life is meant to be happy and trouble free. Like a river, it has rocky patches. Our task is to find a way to cope with inevitable difficulties with "an eye made quiet by the power of harmony," to learn how to remain steady and go with the flow. In truth, the only place of refuge is the silent emptiness within. Meditation helps us to reach this place, to access it even in the worst storms; it reduces life pressure as well as blood pressure.

There is sometimes a misconception that meditation makes people unfocused, spaced out—this could not be further from the truth. It takes much self-discipline to give up a little time each day to meditate. Regular practice permeates all areas of life, making us more focused and efficient in everything we do.

Although it is often associated with Eastern religions, and also Christian mysticism, meditation does not have to be religious in any way. It is a personal experience, one that is open to anybody of any faith, or of none.

The mental, physical and emotional benefits are an enhancement to anybody's life and can fill a spiritual void.

Physical/mental benefits

- Reduced blood pressure
- Relaxed body
- Increased energy
- Mental clarity

Emotional/spiritual benefits

- Calm
- Peace
- Sense of unity
- Compassion
- Detachment

When to meditate

The best time to meditate is between 3 and 5 a.m., when the lungs, which rule our spirituality, have the most energy. Realistically, when you first wake is also a good time, as is last thing at night. Too much or too little sleep hinders meditation and destroys the lucidity needed for one-pointedness. Never meditate after a heavy meal—as with the postures allow two hours after a light snack, four hours after a full meal.

The hardest time to meditate is when you are distressed in some way—and yet taking the time to meditate then is often the key to turning your situation around.

the basic requirements

An experienced practitioner can meditate anywhere—on a train, plane or waiting for an appointment—wherever you have time to spare. However, when you first start meditating, there are four basic requirements.

A quiet place

When, through practice, you gain enough experience you can meditate almost anywhere. When you first begin, however, it helps to find a place where you can be quiet, that has a comfortable temperature and where it is not stuffy. Set the scene by clearing away clutter and lighting candles or incense or burning scented oils.

A comfortable position

Your clothing should not restrict you, so remove belts and ties, undo collars and remove rings, watches or necklaces. Jeans, even stretch ones, are not good for meditation, and take off shoes and socks.

Take a shower before starting, or at least rinse your face and brush your teeth—cleanliness is an important part of yoga practice. And go to the lavatory to empty your bladder and, if possible, your bowels.

If the floor is not carpeted, use a rug for extra comfort, and treat yourself to a meditation cushion, or "zafu." This firm, supportive cushion will be money well spent, as it is more comfortable than the more usual foam blocks. Choose a posture to suit you from those illustrated on these pages.

A passive attitude

Our minds are like butterflies, flitting from topic to topic, restlessly searching for pleasure and satisfaction. They fix on external objects, events and people. We sit and rework old memories, latching on to the good ones, feasting on a daydream as we would a good meal. Or we grumble on internally, chewing the cud of old resentments. I once watched an old lady in a supermarket talking to herself about food choices, the dust on the stairs at home, a child that needed disciplining—she was verbalizing the way most minds work.

Thoughts are like unwelcome visitors turning up to disturb our meditation: and the more we categorize them "good" or "bad" the more power they have to drain our energy. If we leave them uncontrolled they bar the door to inner calm and higher mind states. When you start to meditate, the inner chaos can seem to get louder—in fact, you are just becoming more aware of it.

Developing a passive attitude means learning to let thoughts pass and gently returning your mind to your chosen object. It is unusual for them to disappear altogether, but you can learn to space them out more. Imagine your mind is like a puppy on a retractable leash; when it wanders, gently bring it home. Notice the thoughts and let them float away. Thoughts can teach us, and observing them in this way and identifying regular patterns can bring great insight.

A mental device

It helps to give the mind one thing to focus on, and that used in most forms of meditation is the breath. The beauty is, the more you focus on it, the lighter it becomes, and the more you produce the type of brain waves that settle the mind. In time, you can let go of the mental device and rest in the silent emptiness of the higher mind.

Another ever-present device to focus on is sound. Nadam is the yogic practice of meditation on sound. It is a passive exercise, which transforms in the most powerful way. For highly visual people, it sometimes is more successful to use a candle flame to concentrate on.

SUSKHASANA
Easy pose

Using a firm meditation cushion (zafu) or a foam block, sit on the floor and bend one knee, bringing the foot in toward your inner thigh. Now bend the other knee and bring that foot in front of the first foot. Slide to the front of your cushion or block so that your knees go down. Keep your back straight and the back of your neck lengthened. Place your hands in your lap, one hand lying in the other, thumbs touching, or place them on your knees, palms up and index finger and thumb touching.

Sitting just on the front portion, a zafu cushion allows the knees to relax and hips to open (near left). Sitting on the middle of the cushion (far left) means that the knees are raised and the hips cannot open.

SIDDHASANA
Perfect posture

Here, the right knee is bent with your left heel pulled into the perineum. Your right foot placed so that the heel is against the pubic bone and the foot is tucked into the fold between the calf and thigh of the left leg. (The legs can be reversed if you like.) Place your hands either on your knees or hold them as illustrated in the easy pose (see above), depending on what you find more comfortable.

PADMASANA
Lotus posture

Sit in a cross-legged pose, as in perfect posture (see page 147), but then lift both feet onto your thighs and tuck them in, by pulling on the ankles, soles facing upward. Do not do this pose if one knee remains lifted from the floor or you will be unstable. If you cannot manage the full lotus posture, try a half lotus, as here. Rest the back of your hands on your knees, index fingers and thumbs touching, or place your hands in your lap, as previously described.

EGYPTIAN POSE

Many people assume you must sit on the floor in a cross-legged position in order to meditate properly, but this is simply not true. Realistically, people's bodies vary, and for medical reasons, not to mention old age, it may not be possible, or even preferable, to get down to the floor. Most of us, however, have an ordinary, straight-backed chair available, and one of the classic ways to meditate is to use this to sit in what is known as the Egyptian pose. Sitting toward the front of a straight-backed chair, feet and knees hip-width apart, place your hands comfortably on your thighs above the knees. Keep the spine erect, back of the neck lengthened. Alternatively, lay one hand in the other, thumbs touching.

three simple forms of meditation

These meditations work on all the chakras, but you must keep your spine erect so that they can communicate unhindered. If you feel yourself beginning to slump, straighten up, lengthen the back of your neck and relax your shoulders. Choose the position that affords you the least distraction from discomfort, a pose that you can hold for at least ten minutes (see pages 147–8), and use one of the following meditations. I recommend that you stick with that form for several sessions to give it the best chance to work—and if it works for you, stick with it.

TIPS

❖ Move your attention, if you prefer, to the gentle rise and fall of your breath at your belly—this helps to settle a very active mind, but it can make drowsiness worse.
❖ If you feel yourself becoming drowsy, raise your chin a fraction.

BREATH

1 Sit in a comfortable meditation position (see pages 147–8). Close your eyes, or lower them, and take three deep yogic breaths. Relax.

2 Now take your attention to your breath. Feel the cool air stroking the fine hairs in your nostrils as you breathe in. Feel the warm air on your upper lip as you breathe out. Don't try to manipulate your breathing, just keep paying attention, and when your mind wanders, gently bring it home, back to the breath.

3 Come out of the meditation by opening your eyes, or looking up, when you are ready, and try to maintain the sense of peace.

NADAM
Sound

1 Sit in a comfortable meditation position (see pages 147–8). Close your eyes, or lower them, and take three deep yogic breaths. Relax.

2 Breathing evenly and quietly, focus your attention on incoming sounds.

3 Before long you may become aware of an ever-present sound inside your head. It may be like the hum of a fridge or rushing water. This is the sound of your cells vibrating: nadam. Focus on nadam, and when your mind wanders, gently bring it home, back to nadam.

TIPS

❖ Nadam is often mistaken for tinnitus.
❖ Try not to name the sounds—just listen to each as it appears.
❖ Nadam is very helpful if you have an active mind.
❖ Spending a few minutes on nadam meditation before sleep helps to overcome insomnia.

CANDLE

1 Place a candle on a stool or table in front of you, just below eye level, and light it.

2 Sit in a comfortable meditation position (see pages 147–8) 3 feet (1 m) or so from the candle. Take three deep yogic breaths. Relax.

3 Gaze at the candle flame for a few minutes breathing quietly.

4 Now close your eyes, and try to hold the after-image of the candle flame steady in the center of your forehead for as long as you can.

5 Finish the meditation by opening your eyes when you are ready.

TIPS

❖ If the image of the flame disappears too soon, repeat step 3.
❖ You might need to remove contact lenses before you do this.
❖ This meditation works well for people with a highly developed visual sense.

meditation for the main chakras

This meditation will keep you in touch with, and give you insights about, the health and balance of your seven main chakras. It also helps to stimulate the chakras and enhances communication between them.

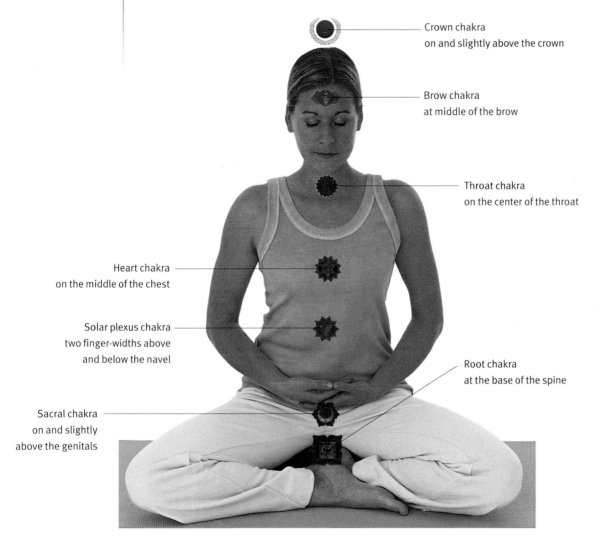

Crown chakra
on and slightly above the crown

Brow chakra
at middle of the brow

Throat chakra
on the center of the throat

Heart chakra
on the middle of the chest

Solar plexus chakra
two finger-widths above
and below the navel

Root chakra
at the base of the spine

Sacral chakra
on and slightly
above the genitals

1 Sit in a comfortable meditation position (see pages 147–8), and close your eyes. Now, take three deep, yogic breaths and relax.

2 For a moment or two focus on Ajna chakra, in the center of your forehead.

3 Now take your attention to each of the chakras in turn, from Muladhara at the base, right up to Sahasrara at the crown, visualizing their color and listening for their sound. Feel open to receiving any messages they might have for you. Become aware of the energy level in each chakra, and any of them asking for particular attention. Use the suggestions to support them in Chapter Two if necessary.

visualizations for the main chakras

I like to make a clear distinction between meditation and visualization. By far, the most important practice to raise energy in the chakras is meditation. However, I have found that visualizations help people to experience the potential of the chakras. Sometimes an individual chakra may feel especially out of balance and may need extra support, but try not to spend too much time focusing on one particular chakra to the detriment of the others, thus creating an imbalance.

MULADHARA
First chakra

1 Sit in the thunderbolt posture (see page 98) and focus on your breath for a few minutes.

2 Now visualize a red light glowing in your perineum. Picture a strong red tap root growing out of the perineum and penetrating deep down into the ground. Imagine the root is anchoring you and nourishing you with all the minerals and nutrients in the soil.

3 Repeat to yourself: "I am grateful for the earth's support. I am secure and unafraid."

4 When you are ready to finish, bring your attention back to your breath, and open your eyes when you are ready.

SVADISTHANA
Second chakra

1 Sit in a comfortable meditation pose (see pages 147–8). Focus on your breath for a few minutes.

2 Now breathe as if right down to your lower abdomen and visualize a basin of clear, bright, orange light glowing in and filling your pelvis. Allow any pleasurable sensations to occur.

3 Stay with the light, breathing quietly, imagining it growing stronger with each out-breath.

4 Repeat to yourself three times: "I welcome and accept all my emotions. My life is full of creative opportunities."

5 Return to normal, quiet breathing and come out of the visualization by listening to the sounds around you. Open your eyes when you are ready.

MANIPURA
Third chakra

1 Sit in a comfortable meditation pose (see pages 147–8), close your eyes and breathe quietly for a few minutes, focusing on the movement of your breath at your navel.

2 Now imagine you are walking, on a glorious sunny day, into the middle of a huge field of sunflowers.

3 Look around you at the golden field, drinking in the sight of all the yellow sunflowers and enjoying the warmth on your body.

4 Your attention is caught by one particular sunflower and, gently holding its bloom in your hand, gaze into its center, feeling the flower's strength and brilliance radiate out toward you.

5 As you gaze into the flower you feel a gradual change, as you seem to become that flower, shining with unique radiance. Enjoy the sensation for a few minutes.

6 Repeat to yourself three times: "I am loving and appropriately powerful."

7 When you are ready, return to a focus on your breath, and come out of the visualization in the usual way.

ANAHATA
Fourth chakra

1 Kneel in the thunderbolt position (see page 98), eyes closed, hands resting on your thighs. Relax your shoulders and concentrate on your breath. Stay with this for several minutes until you are completely relaxed and focused.

2 Next, picture someone you love, who needs healing, kneeling opposite you. Imagine a line of golden light stretching along the floor between you.

3 Now picture this light passing up your backs to join at infinity, establishing a triangle.

4 Ask your higher consciousness (or the divine) at this point that the person may receive healing passing down the light to them. You may receive an image or a message at the point where the light meets, or you may see nothing at all. Either way, give thanks, with complete trust that your friend will receive help.

5 When you are ready, return to a focus on your breath, and come out of the visualization in the usual way.

VISHUDDHA
Fifth chakra

1 Choose a comfortable meditation posture (see pages 147–8), close your eyes and concentrate for a few minutes on your breath.

2 Be aware of the cool air in your nostrils as you breathe in, the warm air on your upper lip as you breathe out. Stay with this for a few minutes.

3 Now take your attention to the sound that the air makes as it passes down your windpipe, and note the slight sound *soh* that it makes as you breathe in and the sound *hum* as you breathe out. Focus on *soh–hum* for a few minutes.

4 Now visualize an intense, turquoise blue light radiating from your throat forward and backward. As you do so, repeat the affirmation: "I trust my inner voice and speak the truth clearly."

5 When you are ready, return to focus on your breath, and come out of the visualization when you are ready in the usual way.

AJNA
Sixth chakra

1 Sit in a comfortable meditation position (see pages 147–8), close your eyes and focus on quiet breathing for a few minutes.

2 Visualize the sun rising in the right hemisphere of your brain, and setting in the left.

3 Now visualize the moon rising in the left hemisphere of your brain and setting in the right.

4 Continue relaxing and visualize radiating indigo light forward out from Ajna chakra.

5 Continue with this image for several minutes.

6 Come out of the meditation in the usual way, and dedicate any insights you might have received to the greater good of all living things.

SAHASRARA
Seventh chakra

1 Sit in a comfortable cross-legged position (see pages 147–8) and breathe quietly until you are completely focused and relaxed.

2 Now visualize a violet light emanating from the crown of your head and projecting upward—the light growing brighter with each breath.

3 Next, picture a white lotus flower in tight bud resting on the crown of your head.

4 As you carry on breathing quietly, visualize the lotus, in the radiance of the violet light, gradually opening a thousand petals until they unfold like a crown upon your head.

5 As you focus on the crown of petals they begin to radiate golden light out into the universe.

6 Stay with this light, connecting you to the universe until you feel ready to come out of the meditation in the usual way.

index

Acknowledgments

I would like to thank the team at Gaia, Hamlyn/Octopus, in particular Jo Godfrey Wood, Patrick Nugent, Camilla Davis, Jennifer Barr and Stella Dwyer for their support and encouragement. I would also like to thank Jonathan Hilton, editor; Peggy Sadler, book design; Elizabeth Haylett of the Society of Authors; Ruth Jenkinson, photographer and her assistant Sarah Bailey; Megan Thomas, model; Victoria Barnes, makeup; Kathie Gill, index; Fred Chance, web design; Janet Swan for her insights on the Chakras and healing; Tim Holland for getting me out of computer blind alleys; Howard Koolman for the reading pile; Rosi Thomas, Stella Barnes, Debby Leek, Anne Gleeson and Francis Hunot for their continued encouragement and for not letting me take myself too seriously; and the indefatigable James McDermott from BT, who went that extra mile to get me reconnected. And last but not least my family, Owen, Megan, Diana, Frank, Nina, Nils and Indigo, for the many insights they give me.

For information on Mary Horsley's Yoga, Meditation, Chakra, and WriteSpace workshops and presentations, contact: www.maryhorsley.co.uk. For information on Mary Horsley's Enneagram workshops, contact: www.enneagramforthespirit.co.uk.

Picture credits

All photographs by Ruth Jenkinson, with the exception of the following:
page 10: akg, London/British Library
page 11: Alamy/Heather Titus/Photo Resource Hawaii
page 18: Corbis UK Limited/David A. Northcott

All illustrations by Bill Donohoe

Editor   Jonathan Hilton
Project Editor   Camilla Davis
Design   Peggy Sadler
Art Direction   Patrick Nugent
Editorial Direction   Jo Godfrey Wood
Production   Louise Hall
Photography   Ruth Jenkinson